Praise for
Flipped

"Instead of taking sides in contentious us-them debates, Doug Pagitt points a way through the tensions to a wider, better place. He uncovers hidden treasures from the Bible and flips conventional understandings. A wise, insightful, and stimulating book!"

—Brian D. McLaren, speaker, author of *We Make the Road by Walking*

"Bravery with kindness can transform—inviting us into new ways of living and thinking. Doug has been doing that in my life for years. *Flipped* is an invitation that so many of us need, offered with bravery and kindness."

—Shauna Niequist, speaker, author of *Bread and Wine* (www.shaunaniequist.com)

"I know of no one more skilled at rigorous and flexible inquiry than Doug Pagitt, who is a masterful and down-to-earth guide to flipped living. *Flipped* presents a vision of faithful Christianity that is hopeful, love-affirming, serious about Scripture, and passionately committed to the way of Jesus."

—Mark Scandrette, founding director at ReImagine, speaker, author of *Practicing the Way of Jesus*

"This is Pagitt at the top of his game . . . and his game is as deadly serious as his title for it is flip. Never has a low-key, conversational tone been more seductively—or effectively—employed in the business of exegetical brilliance than here. This one really is a thought expander as well as a faith enhancer."

—PHYLLIS TICKLE, author of *The Great Emergence*

"Several years ago, I was having another fascinating conversation with Doug. He spoke of his desire that everyone he comes in contact with would know they're loved, they belong, they matter. Doug is obviously extremely intelligent and passionate and articulate, but above all else he has a giant heart of love. That's a rare and much-needed combination, and I'm thrilled to know he's out there doing his thing. The world needs more people like Doug."

—ROB BELL, speaker, author of *The Zimzum of Love*
and *What We Talk About When We Talk About God*

"*Flipped* lets you see that God wants to trespass over the fences we have put on grace and unlock the chains we've put on love. This book is Doug Pagitt's invitation to start afresh with God and not let religious folks hold the Spirit hostage."

—SHANE CLAIBORNE, activist, author of *The Irresistible Revolution*, coauthor of *Red Letter Revolution* (www.redletterchristians.org)

"Doug Pagitt is a fully engaged questioning theologian whose thoughtful teaching and writing illuminate what it means to live in faith."

—SARA MILES, author of *Take This Bread* and *City of God*

"Doug reminds us of just how upside down and powerful the revolutionary call of Jesus can be. *Flipped* will challenge many of your Scriptural paradigms, breathing a fresh freedom and wholeness into your faith as you seek to follow Jesus, the all-time Master of the Flip."

—MIKE SLAUGHTER, activist, speaker, pastor,
author of *Dare to Dream* and *Renegade Gospel*
(www.mikeslaughter.com)

"Doug Pagitt is a lighthearted soul on a serious mission: to help us see the world and ourselves through Jesus's eyes. Reading *Flipped*, I felt a weight I didn't realize I was carrying fall off my shoulders. Read it for yourself. It will change your life."

—THE RT. REV. MARIANN EDGAR BUDDE, bishop
of the Episcopal Diocese of Washington

Flipped

Flipped

The Provocative Truth That Changes
Everything We Know About God

DOUG PAGITT

CONVERGENT
BOOKS®

FLIPPED

PUBLISHED BY CONVERGENT BOOKS

Scripture quotations and paraphrases are taken from the following versions: The Common English Bible. Copyright © 2011 by Common English Bible. The Holy Bible, New International Version®, NIV®. Copyright © 1973, 1978, 1984, 2011 by Biblica Inc.™ Used by permission of Zondervan. All rights reserved worldwide. www.zondervan.com.

Details in some anecdotes and stories have been changed to protect the identities of the persons involved.

Grateful acknowledgment is made for use of the poem "What If?" in *From Yoga Beyond Belief: Insights to Awaken and Deepen Your Practice* by Ganga White, published by North Atlantic Books, copyright © 2007 by Ganga White. Reprinted by permission of publisher.

Trade Paperback ISBN 978-1-60142-637-6
eBook ISBN 978-1-60142-638-3

Copyright © 2015 by Doug Pagitt

Cover design by Mark D. Ford

Published in the United States by Convergent Books, an imprint of the Crown Publishing Group, a division of Penguin Random House LLC, New York.

CONVERGENT BOOKS® and its open book colophon are registered trademarks of Penguin Random House LLC.

Library of Congress Cataloging-in-Publication Data
Pagitt, Doug, 1966–
    Flipped : the provocative truth that changes everything we know about God / Doug Pagitt. — First Edition.
        pages cm
    Includes bibliographical references.
    ISBN 978-1-60142-637-6 — ISBN 978-1-60142-638-3 (electronic) 1. Christian life. I. Title.
    BV4501.3.P333 2015
    248.4—dc23

                                        2014041743

Printed in the United States of America
2015

10 9 8 7 6 5 4 3 2

SPECIAL SALES
Most Convergent books are available at special quantity discounts when purchased in bulk by corporations, organizations, and special-interest groups. Custom imprinting or excerpting can also be done to fit special needs. For information, please e-mail SpecialMarkets@ConvergentBooks.com or call 1-800-603-7051.

In God we live, move, and exist.

—the apostle Paul, in Acts 17:28

Contents

Contents

Introduction

While the title of this book is *Flipped*, I want be clear—or perhaps make a confession. This is a book about Jesus.

I have mixed feelings about writing a book about Jesus. In light of all the prognosticating that has taken place during the last two millennia, I worry that there really is no need for yet another book about Jesus. Second, I realize that people take their view of Jesus very seriously.

There is a chance that I might step on all kinds of land mines. After all, the Flip that is referred to in the book's title is—among other things—a different way to understand Jesus. Beyond that, it leads to a different way to understand the world because of Jesus. I know from experience that not all people take kindly to someone attempting to change their view of Jesus and his teachings.

Even with these worries, or perhaps because of them, I believe Jesus's message has the power to bring about healing of the human spirit, foster life in community, and give us a vision and path for living harmoniously with God and one another.

However, in my thirty-something years in the faith, I have wondered how the provocative, powerful, beautiful message of Jesus ended up producing the kind of religious life I see in the world. And perhaps, like me, you have read the teachings of Jesus and wondered how it led to this.

The question for both of us is, "Does it have to stay this way?"

I believe Jesus was in a similar situation in his day. He wasn't concerned about saying what people wanted to hear. He had no interest in maintaining the status quo. Just the opposite, really. When Jesus spoke, he would deliberately remind people of the officially approved interpretation of Holy Writ. Sometimes he would remind listeners of the Law plus various rules and traditions that guided how people were living.

Then he would switch things up in a way that set the hearers' minds spinning. Just when they thought they knew where he was headed with his message, he spun them around, turned them upside down, and Flipped them over.

Jesus was famous for telling people, "You have heard that it was said . . ." only to turn that bit of common knowledge on its head: "But I say to you . . ." This is Jesus doing what I call the Flip. Just when we think we know where he is taking us, he Flips it over by saying something *much better*. Jesus was not content with leaving things as they were. He wanted change.

Change and growth are what *Flipped* is all about. When Jesus first said the things recorded in the Bible, no one missed his intent. He wanted to change the way they understood God. Of course, many of them were satisfied with the old ways of doing things. They preferred the familiar interpretations and set patterns.

We aren't all that different. We are so used to the words Jesus spoke that we confuse familiarity with understanding. We like to assume that his teachings conform to the accepted interpretation. The opportunity for a Flip can be lost because we rely on what we've always thought he meant.

But Jesus never catered to human assumptions. He and others—Paul, Peter, and John among them—consistently challenged fundamental beliefs and interpretations. Their goal was to change lives and the world.

I am using the Bible as my main point of reference. I know there are great commentaries and studies of the Gospels and the rest of the New Testament. But I wanted to stick with the Bible in order to take a clearer look at what the Gospels say about Jesus. I wanted to look carefully at his words and actions, then try to work out what Jesus was getting at. This is a Bible-heavy book.

If you haven't read much of the Bible, don't worry. I'm not going to go all Greek scholar on you. You don't need to have completed any prerequisites to hear, understand, and live the teachings of Jesus.

If, on the other hand, you are already quite familiar with the Bible and are satisfied with your understanding of all things Jesus, you might be in for a jolt. The teachings of Jesus tend to be most provocative to those of us who feel we've already heard it all before.

Flipped has nothing to do with a quick fix of yourself or the church you're in. It does not recommend leaving the church for some other path to spiritual exploration. Neither is it a manual for setting others straight or a guide to developing a better argument to use against those who differ with your view. You can do all those things without this book and without the unapologetic teachings of Jesus.

Flipped has three goals (and if you find more than these three, go for it).

First, *Flipped* wants you to see that changing your mind, drawing new conclusions, and engaging new ideas all lie at the heart of Jesus's message and life. These are signs of growth. This growth will require you to be curious, open, and engaged. I hope to help you experience firsthand a Flip like none you have encountered before.

Second, *Flipped* wants you to behold the big, beautiful story of God as you find new ways to live in it. You will be invited to hear the apostle Paul make sense of the Jesus story by proclaiming, "In God we live, move, and exist." The life and teachings of Jesus call us to Flip our view from seeing God in us to understanding we live and exist In God.

We live and move In God with our entire self, not just our religious being or our spiritual nature. Living, moving, and existing pretty much covers every microsecond, every atom in our being, every move we make, every aspect of existence. That is the theme that runs throughout *Flipped*.

While this has been part of the Christian story from the start, it has been missed by so many of us. So you will be invited to look at familiar ideas and stories from a new perspective. This will involve some stretching, but that's the point, isn't it? It's almost impossible to hear and see anything differently if you remain committed to familiar patterns. *Flipped* helps you step outside routine ways of thinking long enough to take a completely new look at the meaning of Jesus's words.

Third, and this probably should be listed first, *Flipped* wants to invite you to a full, vibrant life In God. *Flipped* is an invitation to all the goodness and care of God so you will hear the call of God in your life. Use this book as a guide; don't let it become a demand. When it is helpful, lean in and breathe deeply, and if it feels like it is making demands on you that you don't want, lean out.

I hope this book will help you experience the love of God more richly and more fully. I trust that God is at work in you with or without this book. God is love, and love is patient and love is kind and love doesn't demand.

You won't agree with everything you read here. I'm not even sure I have worked out every wrinkle in the themes and truths we will explore. But I trust it will serve as a starting point in accepting Jesus's life and words in a new way.

Are you ready for a Flip?

Getting Flipped

*How Being Turned Upside Down
Makes God Interesting Again*

In God we live, move, and exist.

—Paul, the apostle

Perhaps it has happened to you. You are making your way through life and suddenly find yourself upended by an idea. It's the kind of idea that stays with you and eventually makes a home in your thinking. Over time you can't imagine life without it.

I call this a Flip.

The Flip at the center of this book is one that turned me around as a pastor and a Christian writer as well as in my personal life and faith. I was sideswiped by a notion that caused me to realize God isn't who I thought God was. It's very possible that God is not who you have always assumed God to be. The realization comes to us in different ways.

For me, the Flip came when I was in a hotel room in San Diego and talking with a man I barely knew. My assumptions about the world and how it works were upended.

Sometimes Flips are impossible to ignore. At other times they are so subtle you could easily miss them. You spend the rest of your life trying to understand all that this change means for you and for others. The Flip can take you from being dead certain about an idea or a person or a story to a place where you aren't certain what you believe anymore.

The Flip that hit me in San Diego was like a wasabi shot to the brain.

I should explain that I love wasabi. A lot. Wasabi is a paste made from the stem of a horseradish-like plant. The paste most often is served with sushi, and there is good reason for the combination. The nearly medicinal benefit of the plant is thought to kill bacteria. It goes perfectly with the uncooked fish often served in sushi. My love of wasabi is not for its health benefits, though; it's for the kick. Not just any kick, but a head-snapping, nasal-clearing, eye-widening kick.

While the Flip didn't make my eyes water or my nose run, it did leave me feeling cleaned out, tossed around, and even a little stung. It was as if a direct path connected what I heard to all of my ideas of God, humanity, and what life is all about. I had known before that I didn't have it all straight, but never did

I dream that an encounter with a guy in a hotel room would bring such clarity.

Looking Beyond Our Thinking

It was 2004 and I was one of the organizers of a national pastors' conference. It might seem that life-changing conversations about God would be common in this setting, but these events seem to involve a lot more mundane chitchat than life-altering conversation. In situations where so many people are committed to the religion industry, most conversations stay well inside the boundaries of what we already think. No pastor wants to risk his or her job by crossing too many lines.

But I'm not interested in boundaries. I'd rather see what is possible just outside of what we all think. Curiosity is far more important to our faith than the false security of established certainty.

That might be one reason I liked LeRon almost immediately. He was a respected theologian and one of the presenters at the conference. I sensed he had a lively, curious mind. I was walking by when I heard him say, "And that's when I stopped thinking of God as a separate single subject."

Wait. God is not a separate single subject? God is not separated and removed from humanity? That means . . . And so the Flip began.

It was almost as if I heard one of those Laurel and Hardy double "whoopee" sounds in my head.

God is not a separate single subject. This idea may not strike you with the power it did me. And if I had heard it at another time it might have slid by me without notice. But on this night it hit me hard. It danced with other thoughts that were important to me but seemed out of rhythm with so many of my assumptions about God, humanity, and life.

That's the thing about Flips: once they start, they are almost impossible to stop.

I realized I could think of God in bigger, more integrated, more expansive ways than I had before. I had always felt bound by the more classic descriptions of God. I don't mean the "chummy big guy upstairs" image or the "old man with a white beard" caricature. It was something far more crucial than that.

Prior to this, I had only heard God described in terms of difference and distinction from humanity and creation. The central understanding of God was that God is different. It was as if the important thing about God was that we have absolutely nothing in common with God.

There is this scene in the feel-good movie *Rudy* where Rudy is trying to figure out his life's call. His priest says, "Son, in thirty-five years of religious studies, I've come up with only two hard, incontrovertible facts. There is a God, and I'm not Him." In my past understanding of God, the vast distance between God and humanity was almost a point of pride.

The people I talked to about God in seminary and afterward were convinced that God is, quite simply, Other. But here was

LeRon, a Christian theologian, suggesting that is not the only way to think about God. And, boy, did I want that to be true. Flips don't force us to think in a new way. Rather, they conspire with thoughts that already are in our heads.

I jumped on the idea that if God were not a separate being from all things in the cosmos, then we need not simply say God exists. We can say that God *is existence*. All is In God.

Why This Is Important for Every One of Us

I wanted to live with God directly and passionately. I did not want God to be some distant being that I needed to please. I didn't want to access God only through a system of faith or religion. I didn't want God to be distant at all. But for so long that seemed like a prerequisite for being Christian. You had to begin by believing that God is Other, and then you would follow certain steps to bridge the gap.

I was welcomed into the Christian faith with the understanding that God could live in your heart. I resonated with the personal nature of this: God was as close as my heart. But that was not the full story. I was told I had to adhere to a set of rules if I wanted to make my heart God's home.

But the Flip allowed me to consider that we live in the heart of God rather than the other way around. It took time for me to get comfortable with this understanding. Flips don't immediately settle in and start to feel normal. It takes a while.

This notion of our living in the heart of God may not immediately draw you in. While I am now convinced that it lies at the heart of Jesus's message and even that of the early apostles, I suspect these ideas might make many people nervous. They certainly did me.

It is not essential that anyone immediately embrace a Flip. It is far more important to give it serious consideration. In the weeks following the San Diego conference, I remembered verses I had memorized in my early days as a Christian. These words from the Bible suddenly were saying so much more than I had noticed before. Flips not only open new pathways, but they also help us reconsider what we have become comfortable with.

One of the Bible passages that kept coming back to me was actually a song sung by first-century followers of Jesus. It's recorded in Colossians.

The Son is the image of the invisible God,
    the one who is first over all creation,

Because all things were created by him:
    both in the heavens and on the earth,
    the things that are visible and the things that
        are invisible.
    Whether they are thrones or powers,
      or rulers or authorities,
    all things were created through him and for
        him.

He existed before all things,
>   and all things are held together in him.

He is the head of the body, the church,
who is the beginning,
>   the one who is firstborn from among
>>   the dead
>   so that he might occupy the first place
>>   in everything.

Because all the fullness of God was pleased to live
>   in him,
and he reconciled all things to himself through
>   him—
whether things on earth or in the heavens.
>   He brought peace through the blood
>>   of his cross.[1]

From the start of the Jesus story, people were saying and singing, "All things were created through him and for him. He existed before all things, and all things are held together in him."

Like me, the early followers of Jesus were trying to live beyond the idea that God is in some places but not in others, in some people but not in other people, in some times but not in other times. Rather, all that exists is In God. All things are held together In God. And all of creation is being reconciled or seeking to live harmoniously with God.

Living In God

Over time a passage from the apostle Paul has become one of my favorite constructs for understanding this. Paul said in one of his most famous sermons: "In God we live, move, and exist."[2] I'll say much more about this in the coming chapters, but for now let that idea resonate in you.

In God.

In.

We are *In* God.

What a Flip.

God is not a separate subject that we talk about or relate to through belief, behavior, faith, or practice. Much better than that, God is the very existence of all things. We are called to live congruently within the existence that holds all things together. This notion resonates with beauty, intrigue, majesty, and mystery.

When we are In God and not simply relating to God or serving God or walking with God, we are able to find not only our lives but all parts of our lives in the story of God.

Recently I was talking with some people for whom this was a new idea. Katelyn said, "This reminds me of a conversation I had the other day with a friend who is a Buddhist. She told me the reason she is a Buddhist is that Buddhism has a way to include pain and suffering. I feel like understanding ourselves In God also makes room for that. It seems like nothing is left out."

Katelyn asked several questions about all this, maybe questions similar to ones you have. She said, "I like this idea, but is it really Christian?" I knew right where she was coming from—I have asked myself that same question.

I have come to believe that not only is it Christian, it is the primary understanding of God that we learn from Jesus, Paul, and others. For me, it's the only way that Christianity makes sense.

This book invites you to consider a Flip that makes it possible to live in the heart of God. It can change your understanding of God and the way you live. I'm not suggesting a one-time shift in how you understand a theological idea. Rather, it is a journey of experiencing life In God. I have not yet worked out all the nuances and implications of this Flip. But I have great faith that there is as much to be gained by the act of Flipping as there is to sticking the landing.

When we open ourselves to a Flip, we enter a process of change. We can live, move, and exist as people empowered by the constancy of the love, care, and life of God. That might help explain why Jesus introduced so many of his Flips with the phrase "You have heard that it was said . . ." He was reminding us that, in the past, we were taught to think about God in a certain way.

Then Jesus would introduce a Flip: "But I say to you . . ." The Flip, if you take it to heart, can change your life by changing the way you understand God.

Flipping Out

Change Is Part of Being a Spiritually
Alive Person; Don't Fear It

You have heard that it was said. . . .

But I say to you . . .

—Jesus

L ooking back on my conversation with LeRon, I realize that I
was already primed for a Flip. I had been taking significant
risks in my life and ministry: starting a church, adopting two children, grieving the loss of my father, and joining my wife in the use
of natural-health alternative treatments. So already my categories
had been messed with and my assumptions had been challenged.

But when I started talking to people about the idea that everything is In God, I could tell not everyone loves being Flipped off.

Think about it. Changing your mind gets a bad rap in our

society. When politicians do it, they are labeled flip-floppers. When business people do it, they are wishy-washy and unfocused. When people of faith do it, we are open to accusations of building a house on sand or being backsliders. There is not much commendation built into our common culture when speaking of being a Flipper.

Which is rather strange. We accept and even expect Flipping in all kinds of areas. We encourage our kids to try new foods and beg our friends to listen to new music. We go on social media to share our tastes in books and movies and ideas and cultural movements, thinking that others might be open to trying these experiences as well.

Flipping also sits at the heart of education. We want to learn, to know what we previously didn't know and to live differently as a result. We cheer one another on in these endeavors; we celebrate with ceremonies and awards. Science Flips us almost daily, with new discoveries changing what we eat and the way we think and the way we understand the world. Even the Christian faith is built on a foundation of Flipping—we call it a conversion experience or seeing the light or having an awakening. But only to a point. We welcome the first Flip, the decision to move from a lack of faith to trusting in Jesus. But after that, the second or third or fourth Flip is typically not encouraged.

And yet Jesus and Paul and Peter and John and others were all about the Flip. Of course they didn't call it that. In the Bible, a Flip often is referred to as *repentance*. That word can have a harsh religious ring to it, but it's actually an invitation to a new way of seeing, thinking, and understanding. The Greek word for "repent" is *metanoeo,* which means "to change your mind, to reconsider." Jesus's call to repent was a call to Flip.

One of his most famous tactics was to upend his listeners' understanding of the Law of God. He often used this approach: "You have heard that it was said. . . . But I say to you . . ." I am convinced this preamble is central to Jesus's messages about how we are to live as people who are alive In God. It is fundamental to the way Jesus invites us to see the world, see those around us, see ourselves, and see God.

The Flip is central to a life of faith.

Flip'n Jesus

It doesn't take much digging to see that Jesus uses a variety of approaches to convey the notion of the Flip:

"You must be born anew."

"Believe me when I say . . ."

"Go and learn what this means: 'I want mercy and not sacrifice . . .'"

"Do not worship in temples or on a mountain, but worship in spirit."

"Blessed are the meek."

"Renew your minds."

"Change your hearts and lives, and trust this good news!"

Jesus presented the Flip as change, conversion, growth, development. He declared a new way of living and being. Jesus turned the tables on those selling religion—literally, at times—and called people to a new way of living with a new story in their heads. His teachings can continue to do that with you and me.

When Jesus said those who are poor in spirit are blessed, he compounded the Flip by also mentioning those who mourn, those who are meek, those who hunger and thirst for righteousness, and those who are merciful. Then he continued by mentioning the pure in heart, the peacemakers, and the persecuted. He was not giving us a list of character qualities we ought to try to achieve. He was creating a list of contrasts. The people on Jesus's list were not commonly seen in the first century (or today, for that matter) as being on the side of God. In Jesus's day, the religious establishment believed God was about earthly power, strength, wealth, status. There was a push to keep religion an elite practice, to keep it sacred and holy by keeping it out of the hands of the rabble.

But Jesus didn't see the world that way. He saw the powerless as those who are blessed. And the Flipping continues. We see this when Jesus says,

- "When you pray, don't be like hypocrites."[1]
- "If someone slaps you on the cheek, offer the other one as well."[2]
- "If someone takes your coat, don't withhold your shirt either."[3]

On and on it goes. "*You* are the light of the world"; "*You* are the salt of the earth."[4]

The list goes on. Still, it's easy to miss the Flip. I missed it for a couple of decades. For me, and maybe for you, it was hard to see it because I was looking the other way.

The Flip demands that we seriously reconsider what we've always assumed to be true. When Jesus says to us "I know you have heard that it was said. . . . But I say to you," he is asking us to see a familiar story for the first time. This has all kinds of implications.

The Four-Hour Healing

"Now go home and sleep for four hours, and when you wake up, you should be fine. You should be able to see clearly. If not, give us a call." The aftercare assistant couldn't have been more casual as she said these words. *Oh, okay,* I thought, *so that's a possibility. That's great.*

I had worn corrective lenses since the age of fifteen. Waking in the morning and not being able to read the time on the alarm clock was just the way things were. Growing up I had watched Steve Austin, the Six Million Dollar Man, get a new and improved eye after undergoing a surgical procedure. But I never expected it to happen to me. I was resigned to a lifetime of using external lenses to see. So I was thrilled that I could regain clear eyesight without having lenses perched on my nose.

In 2002 I saved every penny I could and made an appointment to get laser-corrected eyesight. I was shocked at how fast the surgery went. All I needed to do was look into the red light, not move or blink, and after three puffs of air in each eye, it was over. I then closed my eyes and did as instructed. Because I can fall asleep almost any time and nearly anywhere, I arrived home about 3:30 in the afternoon with my eyes covered. I lay down, and in no time I was asleep. When I woke up at 7:17 that night, I was overwhelmed by emotion. It wasn't just that I could read the clock next to my bed or that I didn't have to stumble around looking for my contacts. It was so much more than that. I felt healed, fixed, complete.

I hadn't anticipated this feeling. I didn't feel broken before the surgery; I just needed to put up with wearing glasses or contact lenses. It was an inconvenience more than anything. But upon waking after my four-hour postoperative nap, I felt *healed*. Somehow, it seemed that things were now as they were supposed to be.

Seeing clearly has a powerful effect on a person. What we see is not simply an act of the eye; it is an act of the mind. Our eyes take in light waves, which on their own have no meaning. It is our brains that sort light impulses and make meaning of them. When we see, it is with our brains, with our minds, and with our categories.

Serious Flipping

By suggesting the commonness of the Flip, I don't mean to make light of its importance or the difficulty of change. The process of Flipping is serious business.

Yesterday I was talking with Kylie, a twenty-one-year-old who, for the first time, is spending significant time with a friend who is an atheist. She is beginning to feel that her atheist friend is starting to make sense. She told me that until recently she had never considered that God was anything but real. But now she wonders if God is just a figment of her imagination.

Does she believe in God only because that is what she was told to believe? She can't shake this question.

Kylie's faith-filled friends say she needs to stop hanging around her atheist friend. But she knows there is more to it than that. She knows these ideas are meeting with thoughts that were already in her head.

We rarely are Flipped by an idea that is totally foreign. But when a new idea triggers something we have wondered about in the past, a Flip might be coming.

It is not uncommon to hold on to ideas, convictions, and beliefs that are not useful or helpful. It is simply that the ideas have been with us for a long time and we can't imagine our world without them.

Flips Are Not Easy

I grew up in an apartment complex that had a swimming pool. The pool offered many a rite of passage for us kids. Chief among these was mastering the diving board and achieving a full flip. The diving-board trick was proof that you had the requisite cool-kid skills. From the basic minimum flip you could add your own flair: a dive, a twist, a second flip.

My buddy Cozzie was the first to nail the triple flip, among the greatest accomplishments any of us had witnessed in our ten years on earth. We exploded in cheers as his feet entered the water.

Unfortunately, for me the flip remains an impossible feat. As a kid I was taller than most (I was six feet tall at age eleven), and with my long, under-coordinated body, I just couldn't keep my head tucked. To be honest, the problem was that I *wouldn't* keep my head tucked. The fear of landing on my back made the urge to see the water so strong, I just couldn't stay in the curl.

Diving off the board and executing a complete flip requires you to take your eyes off the water and look to the sky. I couldn't get myself to do it. And I still can't. I have tried to do flips off higher levels, where I had more time in the air, and still I can't do it. As it turns out, it is not the time spent in the air that is the problem; it is the fear in my head that stymies me.

What was true in my body also has been true in other areas of my life and in the lives of many other people. We fear the unpredictability that comes from a Flip. When you go upside down, you lose your points of reference. Up is down and down is up. Many times we resist a new way of thinking or being because it requires losing sight of what is familiar.

There is a famous story of Jesus talking with a man who wanted to know Jesus's secret for living harmoniously with God. The man had succeeded in the ways life is typically measured. He was young, rich, and a ruler. After asserting that he had fulfilled all his religious expectations, he asked Jesus what he could add to his life. Jesus called him to Flip.

"Sell everything you own and distribute the money to the poor. . . . And come, follow me." That was something the man wouldn't do. "The man became sad because he was extremely rich."[5]

I get this guy. Many times I left the pool at my apartment complex doing the classic Charlie Brown walk of humiliation. I knew what it took to complete a flip before hitting the water, but I just couldn't do it.

I understand the difficulty there is in taking the risk of getting upside-down. I empathize with the impulse to walk away when presented with another way of thinking, seeing, and living. When people change, it also can be disruptive to the people around them. There are people in my life who still wonder whether I have lost hold of faith. In fact, it happened again recently. I was writing this chapter at a coffee shop when I ran into a pastor friend I've known for a long time. We chatted a bit, and he asked what I was writing. I told him about Flipping from the idea of God as a separate subject to God being the very existence of all things.

My friend showed signs of being uncomfortable. He said, "Yeah, I really appreciate some of the work you are doing. But you know, I just can't go all the way there with you."

I understand. Flips often make much more sense to the Flipped. Nobody said Flipping was for the faint of heart.

Flipping your thinking is not the same as changing your situation. Your life circumstances can change without a shift in your thinking. My friend Thom works with people transitioning out of prison. Part of his job is to help men stop thinking like prisoners so they can live full lives. Being free is as much a state of mind as a location.

The stories in our heads often influence us more than our circumstances themselves. You see this dynamic at work in people who win the lottery. In an article about a recent Powerball winner in Missouri, Kevin Murphy wrote, "The National Endowment for Financial Education cites research estimating that 70 percent of people who suddenly receive a large sum of money will lose it within a few years."[6]

Flipping in Life

I have gone through a real doozie of a change in addition to my thinking about God. The other change involves my body.

Two years ago I was not a runner. At all. I used to be a college basketball player and have been playing recreational ball for the last twenty-five years. My willingness to run was limited to getting from one end of the court to the other.

Before two years ago, I had run three miles exactly once in my life. That was only because I was part of a fundraiser for a friend's nonprofit organization. And I hated it. Upon finishing that 5K, I said to my friend, "Please, next time let me just write you a check and never make me do that again."

At the time of this writing I have been running for twenty-three months. And I have really gotten into it. I have run a lot: one 5K, three half marathons, six marathons, one thirty-one-mile ultra-marathon, two fifty-mile ultra-marathons, and a twenty-four-hour run during which I covered eighty-five miles.

And I have loved every step of every race.

To put it mildly, in the last two years I have become a runner. I experienced one of my classic Flips.

It all started by accident. In January 2012 I had finished a thirty-day juice-only diet and had lost thirty pounds. I was starting to feel really healthy. Prior to this I had struggled with a chronically sore calf muscle that I was constantly pulling during basketball games. I wondered if the weight loss combined with some strengthening I had been doing might have solved the problem. I got on a treadmill to test my calf. I started walking, then trotting, then slowly running. My goal was to see how long I could go until I felt the familiar twinge of pain. I was surprised after ten minutes that my leg felt good. At thirty minutes my calf had not started to hurt and I was just plain bored, so I decided to stop.

A few days later I decided to really put my legs to the test. After six miles of walking, trotting, and running, I decided my calf was indeed strong and healed. I thought nothing more of it beyond posting on Facebook that I went for six miles on a treadmill and my calf held up. Anna commented on my post: "If you went six miles on a treadmill, then you are ready for a half marathon. You should run the Get Lucky with us on March 17." I said to myself, *I should totally run that half marathon*. In an act of novice ignorance, I clicked on the link she posted, paid my sixty-eight dollars, and was signed up for a half marathon that would take place in ten short weeks.

I didn't know the slightest thing about running a half marathon, so I started clicking around the Internet to find a training plan. I mentioned to people that I was planning to run a half marathon in two and a half months. I was met with the appropriate questions: "Are you crazy?" "When did you become a runner?" "You know you are going to hurt yourself going that far so soon, right?"

I started to wonder if my weight loss had given me an unrealistic perspective on myself. What made me think I could go 13.1 miles in the winter just two and a half months from now? I started to worry as I thought about the story of Pheidippides, who in the legend of Marathon, ran twenty-six miles to announce the end of a war and died just after sharing the news. I wondered if running half of a death sentence could possibly be good for me.

Born to Run

Many of my running friends recommended a book titled *Born to Run*. As a diehard Bruce Springsteen fan, I was immediately interested. As it turns out, the book has nothing to do with the greatest poet and songwriter in the world, but rather, as the subtitle puts it, the book is about *A Hidden Tribe, Superathletes, and the Greatest Race the World Has Never Seen*.

Three days after signing up for the race, I downloaded the book and listened to it from beginning to end on a drive from

Minneapolis to Chicago and back. Little did I know I was about to repent, think anew, and become a runner before ever running a training mile.

Contrary to the thoughts I had about the dangers of running, author Christopher McDougall makes the case that human beings are the perfect running animals. We are not the fastest, but we can run the farthest. With deft storytelling and excursions into biology, anatomy, and history, this book gave me an alternative to the running story that had been stuck in my head.

I had experienced running as a means to an end—getting from one end of a basketball court to the other. I also had seen running as a means of punishment. In sports my coaches used running laps or sprints as punitive motivation. "Pay attention or you will start running," my basketball coaches would bark. "If you keep screwing around in practice," my football coach would say, "you will spend the rest of practice running laps."

In sixth grade, my gym class had to go through a week of testing for the presidential fitness test. We had to do pull-ups and sit-ups, then try to climb a rope to the gym's ceiling. Plus we had to do the dreaded half-mile run. As an unusually big kid, this was a nightmare scenario. I couldn't do a pull-up, and there was no way I could run twice around that huge track. My body size and muscle development were on totally different schedules.

It was embarrassing and caused me to curse President Ford all the way around the track. There were so many reasons I didn't like running, and my body was only part of the reason. My mind was most of it.

Becoming a runner was only in small part a change in my body; it was almost entirely a change in my thinking. That's what happened on the car trip while listening to the story of the Tarahumara people of northern Mexico, one of the world's great running tribes.

Up until then I had believed what I was told, that the human body can run only so far, and then running becomes unhealthy. For the bulk of the twentieth century, running long distances was considered a potentially dangerous activity. So much so that the Olympics did not include a women's marathon until 1984, in part because it was believed it was too dangerous for women to run that distance. It was even suggested in the 1970s that a uterus could fall out from running twenty-six miles![7] Such wild tales of death and injury had helped create my mindset of the danger of running long distances. It was in my head that the reason I didn't like running was because it was unnatural and even dangerous. So when *Born to Run* suggested just the opposite, that humans are born to run and to run really far, it grabbed me as an alternative story.

McDougall suggests that when we look at the persistence of hunters on the African plains today, we see our biological heritage. These hunters kill antelope not by shooting arrows or making traps, but by running the animals to death. These men are skilled trackers who can run down an antelope in four hours. (You can watch a BBC documentary showing the San people of the Kalahari Desert doing just that.[8])

The human body is made to run. Really, really far. Humans

are the only animal who can breathe at a different rate from our heart rate. This means humans can keep running without jeopardizing their hearts. Their prey can't do this, so if the hunter can keep the animal running, it will ultimately die of a heart attack.

This way of hunting matters because it answers an important question in the evolutionary biology of human beings. There is a bit of a puzzle regarding how our early human ancestors developed larger brains. It is understood that the brain development of early hominids was the result of eating animal protein some two million years ago. The dilemma is that humans didn't develop weapons and traps until some two hundred thousand years ago. So how did our earlier ancestors obtain a steady diet of animal protein without trapping or shooting their prey? The answer: they ran them to death.

While driving and listening to this in *Born to Run*, it struck me that running long distances was not a death sentence; it was what gave our species life.

With this new life-not-death story in my head, I got home and immediately set out on the first seven-mile run of my life. I felt so inspired by that run that the next morning I registered for the American River Fifty Mile Endurance Run, just fifteen months away.

I was now, in my mind, a runner. In fact, I even believed I was born to run. Not because I had yet run all that far or often, but because in my mind a new reality had set in.

Over the last two years I have been on a constant learning curve. I have changed my stride, built muscle and strength, and worked hard on diet and nutrition. Most important, I have changed my thinking. There is a saying in the ultra-marathon world (an ultra is any distance over 26.2 miles): "Running an ultra is 80 percent mental, and the other 20 percent is all in your head."

There is no doubt that running for eight, twelve, twenty-four, or thirty-five hours is a great physical feat, but it is not primarily about muscles, lactic acid, stretching, and stride. It is mostly about the story in your head.

The story in our heads affects the acts of our feet. The early Christians had this sense. They wanted to not just tell a slightly different story of God; they wanted everyone to know that there is nowhere we can go to be outside of God: "Nothing can separate us from God's love in Christ Jesus our Lord." "In God we live, move, and exist." We are In God. And we can "be transformed by the renewing of [our] minds."[9]

So it goes with all our Flips: a new story is the start to reshaping our lives In God.

What It Means to Live, Move, and Exist

How Living In God Makes All the Difference

Nor is God served by human hands, as
though he needed something, since he is the
one who gives life, breath, and everything else.

—Paul, the apostle

M any of us think of Paul only as the great apostle. But, in
addition, he was a fractious figure in the early history of
Christian faith. Paul was originally a persecutor of those who held
to Christian faith. It was a time when both the faith (the Way)
and the man (Saul, a zealous Jew) went by different names. Saul
was a Pharisee. Pharisees were part political party, part social

movement, part school of thought. Above all, they were committed to the preservation of a belief system that connected God closely with the temple in Jerusalem.

Saul arrested and even killed people who were charged with blaspheming against the official temple-based Jewish teachings. But this Pharisee among Pharisees hit a turning point. The story goes that Saul was struck blind, heard the voice of Jesus calling him to stop persecuting people who were following the Way, and to instead become a follower of it. Talk about a Flip.

Saul went through not only a name change, to Paul, but a life change as well. His newly Flipped life took him out on the road to spread the new understanding of God that he previously had sought to destroy.

Paul's Flip toward life In God created waves around the world, waves that still threaten to knock us off our feet today. One of his travels took him from Jerusalem all the way to Greece. An area of Athens was called the Areopagus. It was the center of thought exchange for much of the known world. Great thinkers would come there to debate the big ideas of life, religion, government, philosophy, sexuality, and humanity. It was the well-educated global melting pot, a fast-changing area of the ancient world. The Romans referred to the Areopagus as Mars Hill, renaming it after one of their gods—the god of war.

It is said that there was not an idea with any currency that wasn't bantered about at the Areopagus. It was the place where the voices of the masses would coalesce into great thinking.

The story of Paul's time at the Areopagus is told in great detail in Acts 17. He had walked around the city, noticing idols everywhere he looked. Idols, both then and now, are the perfect representation of a transactional religious system. In the first century, an idol was not thought of so much as a god but rather as a means by which people could connect with the gods. Idols were the means of a sought-after religious transaction.

Paul was convinced that the life and resurrection of Jesus meant that God was fully accessible to all of humanity without a go-between. So when he toured this great city and saw a complex industry of transactional religion, he called on the philosophers to think again. He wanted them to Flip by putting an end to the need for idols, temples, and any other system of transaction. There was a new story for them to live in.

Paul stood up in the middle of the council on Mars Hill and said, "People of Athens, I see that you are very religious in every way. As I was walking through town and carefully observing your objects of worship, I even found an altar with this inscription: 'To an unknown God.' What you worship as unknown, I now proclaim to you. God, who made the world and everything in it, is Lord of heaven and earth. He doesn't live in temples made with human hands. Nor is God served by human hands, as though he needed something, since he is the one who gives life, breath, and everything else.[1]

In many ways Paul was contrasting the Jewish story with the Athenians' fascination with idols. The Jewish people had long been committed to offering an alternative to idols with the story of the living God. You can almost hear Paul harkening to the Creation story, with God giving breath to all living things. God "gives life, breath, and everything else."[2]

Then he really brought the message home: "God isn't far away from any of us. In God we live, move, and exist."[3]

"In God we live, move, and exist" is a fascinating statement, and as it turns out, it's not original to Paul. He was quoting Epimenides, a sixth-century BCE poet who had originally written this about Zeus. Paul may well have known of its earlier reference and didn't care. He knew that "in God we live, move, and exist" was true. He contended that this truth was best told by the life of Jesus and not the story of the mythological Zeus. God is not out there; God is not something we can represent in a handmade object. Rather we live, move, and exist In God. This is an all-encompassing understanding of God.

This was a Flip for the thinkers who heard Paul say these things. And it's a Flip for most of us today, even those who are familiar with Paul's famous sermon in Athens. Given how seriously his teachings have been studied for hundreds of years, it is shocking to me that this early message of Christianity is still so foreign to so many of us.

Paul went on to play out this idea by suggesting that God does not need nor want anything from humanity, but rather that the fullness of humanity exists In God. He then argued that this was shown by God's raising Jesus from the dead. Beyond that, the power of God that was alive in Jesus is alive in us. In short, the fullness of God is active in humanity without assistance from any religious system.

Paul continued,

Therefore, as God's offspring, we have no need to imagine
that the divine being is like a gold, silver, or stone image
made by human skill and thought. God overlooks
ignorance of these things in times past, but now directs
everyone everywhere to change their hearts and lives.[4]

I hear Paul echoing the Jesus-style saying "You have heard that it was said. . . . But I say to you . . ." As the apostle spoke to the Athenians, it went something like this: "I know you have heard it said that you must get to God through idols, but I say to you, 'Don't think about God as some distinct, separate subject, but rather repent, change your thinking, Flip, and see the fullness of humanity In God and the fullness of God in humanity as it is expressed in Jesus.'"

It was a provocative thing to say. Paul's recommended Flip was met with varied responses. For some, it rang true like an ancient rhythm. But others sneered and called him a babbler and a fool.

The fullness of God existing in humanity ran counter not to just one religious group's sensibilities but to nearly all who advocated a transactional approach to God. Most religious structures have a lot to gain by seeing God as a being distinct from all of creation. By characterizing God as the divine entity on the far side of a chasm, the religion can then offer a way to bridge the gap.

It does take some getting used to, this idea that God does not simply exist, but that God *is* existence. Everything is In God.

I now see God through the lens of integration. It has allowed me to reorient not only my view of myself but also of other people. Flipping my understanding from "God is in me" to my being In God has opened up new ways of viewing others. I no longer have to wonder if people may not have God in them or that they may not know what they need to be connected with God or that some behaviors or actions disqualify them from living well with God.

It is freeing to not have the responsibility of serving as arbiter of who has access to the richness of God's love and goodness. Instead, we can recognize that all people live, move, and exist In God. We all are called to live wholly with God regardless of where we are in any process of understanding. There is such freedom in not needing to fulfill any prerequisites to merit a life with God.

The Bigness of Living In God

God is far bigger than I ever imagined. When everything is In God, it simply isn't possible to hold on to a small view of God.

A review of English usage can help clarify this Flip. You may recall that a preposition is a word that links nouns, phrases, and pronouns to other words. Prepositions are words such as *over, across, after, by, into, on, to,* and *under.* The English Club puts it like this:

> There are about 150 prepositions in English. Yet this is a
> very small number when you think of the thousands of
> other words (nouns, verbs etc.). Prepositions are impor-
> tant words. We use individual prepositions more frequently
> than other individual words. In fact, the prepositions **of,**
> **to** and **in** are among the ten most frequent words in
> English. . . . Many of these prepositions have more than
> one meaning.[5]

In English, the meaning of words depends on their context and the words they relate to. The surrounding words matter a lot. For many who pick up English as a second or third language, parsing prepositions is hard work. Mastering the separate mean-ings of *in, on,* and *at* can present a challenge.

Talking about the power of small words calls to mind verb tenses and the impeachment hearings of president Bill Clinton. The hearings included the president's testimony in front of a grand jury in which he bickered over the meaning of the word *is.* He was asked if he had allowed his attorney to make "a completely false statement" about Clinton's relationship with intern Monica Lewinsky. (The attorney had said, "There is absolutely no sex of any kind in any manner, shape, or form.") Clinton's response to the question was that the attorney's statement was true at the time it was made.

The president said, "If someone had asked me on that day, are you having any kind of sexual relationship with Ms. Lewinsky, that is, asked me a question in the present tense, I would have said no. And it would have been completely true."

He earlier had said, "It depends on what the meaning of the word *is* is."

The president was stressing the distinction between *is* (present tense) and *was* (past tense). While it's true there is a great difference in verb tenses, his explanation did not sit well with the American public. No one likes the smart-aleck wordsmith guy.

Comedian Demetri Martin does a standup routine that points out idiosyncrasies of the English language. He quips, "Why, when we meet someone in person, do we say, 'I'm Demetri Martin,' while on the phone we say, '*This is* Demetri Martin'?" He points out how odd and hilarious it would be to answer the phone saying, "*I am* Demetri" and when meeting someone to say, "*This is* Demetri Martin."[6]

When I talk about all of creation being *In* God, I'm not just using a turn of phrase. As we have noted, the choice of preposition sends a specific meaning. Paul stated that *In* God we live, move, and exist. He did not say "with God" or "at a distance from God." The preposition *in* is a profoundly meaningful word. And flipping the order of words from "God is in all" to "all is In God" is more than a semantic move. It offers us a clearer, more honest, more biblical understanding of who God is and who we are In God.

Some Things Are Hard to Say

A Flip of this magnitude bears close scrutiny. "So if God is in everything," said seventeen-year-old Nathan, "this Cheeto is God, then?" He shook a dried, cheese-covered cornmeal snack in his mom's face. This was not the first time Carole had been confounded by her teenage son. Nathan liked to use his quick wit and sharp tongue to expose what he considered to be his mom's lapses in logic.

Since Carole's spiritual renewal, she had been finding new ways to talk about God, life, and faith. Like many people new to faith, she was looking for language to use when talking about God, but often it felt awkward. What she knew of God from popular culture and religious instruction was of little use: "The big guy upstairs," "God as the universe," "God as personified humanity." None of these phrases, or even the pronoun *he,* got at what she was experiencing with God. She was living something life giving and fresh in her spirit and relationships. Almost every time she tried to put words around her experiences, the words fell short.

When we lack the words to talk about God with nuance and dynamism, the situation is ripe for overstatement, which often leads to argument. We need not just new words but also new concepts of God in order to talk about God in ways that fit with our experience of God.

Carole doesn't see herself as a philosopher or theologian. She is an artist. She's not interested in complex ideologies or word games, which seem to entertain religious theoreticians. But she does take new understandings of God seriously. She knows that the story running through your head forms and shapes how you live, how you approach spirituality, and how you view humanity.

During the Cheetos conversation with her son, she found herself at a loss. She wanted to affirm her conviction that God is everywhere and present in all things. When her teenager brought out a Cheeto, Carole, in a moment of exasperation, shouted, "Yes! God is in the Cheetos. God is in everything." She knew instantly that was not what she wanted to say. It didn't make sense even to her, but neither did the alternative. Is there any place or anything that is void of God?

Even to say that "God is in everything" still doesn't quite get to it. Carole can tell you that four years later, now enjoying a great relationship with her son, the conversation has not left her. She is still working on these ideas. She is still trying to find a way to say there is no boundary to God *and* Cheetos are not God.

Carole's predicament is shared by many of us. We wonder, *What's the value of a God who is indistinguishable from me, you, this tree, a computer keyboard, or a bag of chemically altered corn snacks?* For most people, not much.

So when Carole wants to convey that there is a God and she doesn't want to pitch the notion of a distinction-based transactional religion, she ends up granting way too much importance to a cheesy corn snack. The overstatement seems better than an understatement when talking about the nearness of God.

A Better Alternative

What if overstatement is not the only choice? What if there is another way to think about God, humanity, and existence—a way that may strike some as new but has been around for as long as humanity? a way of living with God that has competed against the transactional understanding from the start?

There is language that begins to capture the reality that has been there all along.

God does not exist; God is existence

In many expressions of faith there is a sense of the oneness of God as very existence. We do not exist apart from God; we exist In God. God *is* existence. Not only is this the story arc of the Bible's narrative, which we will get to in a moment, but it shows up in other faiths as well.

Jay Michaelson has written about how talking about God not as an object but as the existence is hard as it relates to nondualistic Judaism:

> This is not because of a desire to be mysterious, but because language denotes; it describes; it marks and distinguishes one thing from other things; and it is part of the social community that created it. Yet if language is inherently dualistic, and inherently social, it is inherently incapable of describing that which is not an object to which one might refer, and which is not other than oneself.[7]

The philosophical name for a distinction-based understanding of God is often called dualism. It is the notion that the world is composed of distinct parts: God and creation, spirit and flesh, matter and energy. The power of dualism extends even into the ways we talk about ourselves. We are comfortable describing our bodies as if they are something other than us. "My foot hurts" is a functional statement, but it indicates a dualism that designates my foot as separate from my person. I would be better off saying, "I hurt, and I feel that hurt in a part of the whole that is me. It's the part of me often referred to as the foot."

But who wants to have coffee with a guy who talks like a Yoda wannabe? So I simply say, "My foot hurts." But it's important to not allow speaking in shorthand to make us think that somehow our foot is not also us.

This brings us back to Christian faith, going all the way back to Jesus's time on earth. That is where we find the best and most clarifying thinking about living and existing In God. And to go back further, we need to look at the spiritual heritage of Christianity dating back to Abraham.

The Call In

Paul's move away from the temple system into the human system was revolutionary: "God, who made the world and everything in it, is Lord of heaven and earth. He doesn't live in temples made with human hands."[8]

Even the Greeks and Romans knew that the Jewish story had

a temple, and most faiths had temples of some kind. I don't know much about temples and religious systems that utilize holy buildings, but I do understand systems that use temple metaphors in powerful ways.

A Catholic church along one of my running routes has these words carved into the stone over the front door: "The gateway to heaven . . ." This idea comforts those who like to think there are places that serve as gateways or portals to the spiritual or divine. Churches, shrines, and other religious structures can send a message that something special happens there that does not happen across the street at Starbucks.

It is easy to understand an impulse that tells a person that all in the world is not as it is supposed to be, but there are special places here and there where all is right with God. Hie thee to a holy place, to borrow from the Bard.

The religious movement known as Eckankar has its world temple and headquarters a few miles from my house. Some of my friends worked for the construction company that erected the building. They had to sign agreements pledging they would not enter the building after it was constructed since it would be consecrated to become more than a building. It would be a temple, and the construction workers would not qualify for entrance. Places built by humans for the purpose of spiritual connection can't help but limit the participation of humans. This is not unique to new religious movements.

I experienced something similar visiting Buddhist temples in Thailand. I was part of a group that had a chance to talk with monks at a rural temple in Lopburi. Our group was invited to sit on the raised floor with the monks, but the women from our group, as well as local women from the town, needed to stay off the raised platform area. Instead, they had to squeeze in between the raised area and a wall.

I noticed that the women from the village who were our hosts didn't approve of this rule. They kept inching closer to the platform where the men were sitting. When someone from our group asked why only men were welcomed to sit on the platform, the monks told us that gender-based rules were enforced in the temples. Women, they said, are not right for the platform.

In any classic, limited, transactional system, some people are allowed to do things that others are not. And sometimes this limited If/Then view can seem to be just what the Bible requires. There are all these times in the Hebrew Scriptures when the text seems to spell out a precise If/Then call. The Old Testament is not a single story, but rather a collection of stories told over many years and from differing perspectives. Part of the dynamism of the collection of thirty-nine books is that there are two major groups framing and writing the text: priests and prophets. The trajectory of the Christian faith has been to follow the lead of the prophets and of Jesus and to bring an end to the If/Then demands.

The priests operated a transactional If/Then system based on ceremonial laws and temple requirements. The prophets called for an end to this. In the Hebrew Bible you see the contrasting views clearly. There is a temple-based system of animal sacrifice, which included strict rules about who could enter certain holy places and who was qualified to perform specific holy acts. I have seen similar limiting customs enforced in Christian, Muslim, and contemporary Jewish traditions. Meanwhile, the prophets were calling for an end to ritual sacrifice. They quoted God in saying "I desire faithful love and not sacrifice, the knowledge of God instead of entirely burned offerings."[9]

In some Christian traditions the impulses of distinction are more subtle than the "men here, women there" practice at a Buddhist temple in Thailand. I visited a church that met in an elementary school and had a rock band. The pastor wore jeans and the attendees sat at lunchroom tables. It was about as far from a traditional temple as you could get. I met with the pastor later, and he told me people could sit wherever they like, but the church is particular about who can play in the band or speak from the stage. To have a role up front, a person has to first demonstrate a certain level of faithfulness.

In many ways the front stage at this nontraditional church is just as limiting as the raised platform of the Buddhist temple. Both limit access based on the notion that some people are different from others and therefore have a different connection with God or no connection. Distinctions can be based on gender or belief or faithfulness or some other transaction.

I have friends who work in religious systems that may not distinguish the holy places in the building from the ordinary places, but they do make a distinction to determine who can do what. They have rules governing who speaks the words before communion and who is authorized to administer the water of baptism. For some these are just organizing principles and part of their tradition, but for others they are connected to assumptions of distinction and difference.

Religious dogma and practice introduce novel ways to keep God at a distance and us in pursuit of a supposedly distant God. You would think that religion serves the purpose of convincing us that God is as finicky and easily bothered by the wrong people as we are. It's easy to see that in any transactional system, we fashion God in our own image. We feel more comfortable when limits are imposed, so we devise a way for God to endorse the limits we prefer.

Paul told the philosophers in Athens, "God, who made the world and everything in it, is Lord of heaven and earth. He doesn't live in temples made with human hands. Nor is God served by human hands, as though he needed something, since he is the one who gives life, breath, and everything else."[10] According to this argument, the God of the former killer of Christians is more welcoming and accepting than the gods of the intellectuals of ancient Greece.

It Is About Integration, Not Connection

The question to pursue is not "In whom or in what does God reside?" Rather, we need to ask "How integrated are we with God?"

If you have ever felt out of sorts with yourself, you know what it's like to be in your body but at odds with it. Integration is not about proximity; it's about harmony. Today, in my yoga class, I was working on opening my right hip. The instructor came over and placed his hand on my left hip to help keep it on the ground. He said, "Sometimes you have to help your body remember how to work well with itself." It was a reminder that sometimes we need some assistance to live in harmony even with ourselves.

We all have lived at odds with God even though we are In God. In fact, it is because we are In God that we are called to live in ways that are harmonious with God. The same Paul who penned the words above later wrote,

> I have the freedom to do anything, but not everything is
> helpful. I have the freedom to do anything, but I won't be
> controlled by anything. . . . Or don't you know that your
> body is a temple of the Holy Spirit who is in you? Don't
> you know that you have the Holy Spirit from God, and
> you don't belong to yourselves?[11]

There is a great prayer in a letter from Paul to followers of the In-God Jesus-life that captures my hope for all of us as we live, move, and exist In God.

> I kneel before the Father. Every ethnic group in heaven or
> on earth is recognized by him. I ask that he will strengthen
> you in your inner selves from the riches of his glory
> through the Spirit. I ask that Christ will live in your hearts
> through faith. As a result of having strong roots in love,

I ask that you'll have the power to grasp love's width and length, height and depth, together with all believers. I ask that you'll know the love of Christ that is beyond knowledge so that you will be filled entirely with the fullness of God.

Glory to God, who is able to do far beyond all that we could ask or imagine by his power at work within us; glory to him in the church and in Christ Jesus for all generations, forever and always. Amen.[12]

God Without the Adapter

*Flipping the Religious Requirements
That Stand Between You and God*

Worship the Father neither on this
mountain nor in Jerusalem. . . .
Worship God in spirit and truth.

—Jesus

I have a basement full of adapters. Boxes of them. Crates. And to be honest, drawers full of them. If there were a support group, I would proudly be there, saying, "I'm Doug, and I have a lot of adapters."

I take some solace in knowing that I am not the only one. It seems to be a guy thing. Well, really a middle-aged guy thing. Many guys I know have a huge collection of old cords and adapters. Some keep them in bins in the basement like I do; others stash them in a kitchen drawer or in a plastic bag at the office. In most cases we don't even have the camcorder, computer, DVD player, VCR, phone, or camera that once benefitted so greatly from these little adaptive gems. So why do we still have the adapters?

There seems to be some kind of emotional memory attached to these wires with their oddly shaped, special-purpose ends. Perhaps we carry with us the trauma of the time we couldn't connect the camera to the TV to show our relatives highlights of our vacation. Or perhaps we recall how much we spent on that special cord and convince ourselves that it must still be worth something to someone.

The problem is that every device comes with its own unique adapter. Even two different generations of the same smart phone or computer can have different cords and adapters. And the adapters often fail before the device, meaning we can end up with two or even three cords for every piece of equipment. They are unreliable and endlessly frustrating, but it seems we can't get by without them.

Does God Require an Adapter?

If we want to transfer electricity from a source to a device, we need the right adapter. If we want to transfer data from one device to another, we have to have the necessary adapter.

Adapters are big business in the electronics world. And the notion of an adapter is really important in the religion world. This is due to the idea that God is distant and completely unlike us.

Understanding God to be wholly Other—distinct from and incompatible with humanity and creation—is problematic because, like an old boom box, for the religious system to work, you have to have an adapter. Want to connect with God? Hunt around for the right cord, plug, and jack combination that will transfer knowledge of God into your spirit. If we are one kind of thing and God is another, there can be no relationship between the two without making use of an authorized intermediary.

The assumption that you and I can't possibly hope to connect with God on our own is built into nearly every doctrine and structure we have inherited from religious teachings and experiences. Like a bin full of cords, we have religious adapters: prayer, church, the Bible, and more. Our theologies are built around the notion that we have to create a connection between two unlike entities. I call this way of thinking about God the transactional approach to faith.

But the adapter is only one part of the solution. Following the act of making a connection, there needs to be some interaction or engagement. The one thing must affect the other. The goal is connection and communication. The obstacle is the incredibly unlike natures of the two entities to be connected.

This is where we run into trouble. If God is wholly Other, how can humans rig the system to get something out of God? If there is a set way to do this, who can explain it and who ends up managing it?

The good news that we see in Jesus is God with humanity. The good news we hear from Paul is that we live, move, and exist In God. We can live without a religious adapter.

Transactional Analysis

Managing the transaction between God and humanity has been the function of religious systems for much of human history. I would even suggest that religious systems benefit most from people believing that human connection with God requires an approved transactional system.

Like the credit-card processing company that moves money from your bank account to pay a bill, there is big money in being in the transaction business. And there is great competition between transactional systems. If you have been part of a theological conversation where people advocate different actions that will or won't result in salvation, you know what competition can do.

There is something dehumanizing about transactional approaches to faith. And ironically, they are not very good for God either. A transactional approach shifts the power from God and from the individual and invests it in the adapter. The spiritual search is reduced to working out the right technical specifications. You need to have the right plug at each end, the correct cord to link the plugs, and a proper jack at each end to receive the plugs. With both entities distinct and completely other, the success or failure of a connection relies on the adapter. If you should mess up and bring along the wrong adapter, you can't complete the transaction. You'll get nothing but silence.

This is not unlike the frustration I experience when I can't remember the password for my ATM account, so I can't get hold of cash when I need it. I have been banking at the same bank for twelve years. Recently I received the news that it was bought by a new financial-services group. As part of the corporate transition, customers were issued new ATM cards with predetermined PIN codes. These codes could not be changed without my going into a local branch. Having not been inside a bank branch since the last time we cashed in the coins from our loose-change jar, I felt I could bypass the bank visit by using the new PIN. I went weeks being frustrated every time I entered the code incorrectly. I couldn't escape the realization that my money was not available to me because I couldn't remember a secret code that someone at the bank told me I had to use.

I was frustrated enough to look for a new bank, which I will do as soon as I have time to go into a branch to fill out the required paperwork. Now multiply the frustration caused by the screwed-up process for getting to your cash with a person's feeling limited when it comes to gaining access to God.

Transactional Systems Are Built on Scarcity

I do a lot of my writing from an award-winning patisserie in south Minneapolis. There are fifty-eight places for people to sit. There is a display filled with the most luscious, savory baked goods and confections you could imagine. The staff is made up of master espresso and coffee curators. I love this place. There is never a shortage of sugary delicacies.

But there is a shortage of electrical outlets. There are only three in the entire sitting area. So for those who have to function with a failing computer battery, a seat near these outlets is at a premium. I've spent enough time here that I know when these seats are most likely to be available, so I plan my day accordingly. When I walk in and find the power-outlet spaces available, I count myself one of the lucky ones.

It is a classic scarcity situation. The solution to my power needs can be met, but only when the conditions are right. I have a visceral emotional response when I get a table by an outlet. The scarcity of outlets creates longing, desire, anticipation, gratitude, and a sense of achievement. These are powerful feelings, enough to lead me to alter my behavior and arrange my life in such a way that I get to enjoy the benefits of claiming an outlet.

Every now and then, however, I get there, and after snagging my premium spot, I open my bag and realize I've forgotten to bring my power cord. The disappointment is far worse than not getting a seat at an outlet table in the first place. I'm so close and yet so far. No matter how freely the electricity is flowing into the outlet, I can't make a connection without having the right custom cord.

Far too often the Christian faith relies on a similar sense of scarcity to pull people into churches. If a church can convince you that what they offer is superior to the competition and available only to those who are in the know, they can play on your longings and desires. An atmosphere of scarcity is essential. "You can't go just anywhere if you want to benefit from these traditions and this use of religious language and our set of required practices. You can benefit from these things only if you are present here with us." The scarcity approach builds longing, anticipation, and gratitude among those who seek a connection with God.

The church serves as the required adapter. "You want to connect with God? Of course you do. Come next Sunday and we'll get you plugged in."

Transactional Systems Rely on the If/Then Principle

When I was an eighth grader in 1979, I was told that understanding computer code was the key to future success. So not only did my schoolmates and I have to take typing class, but we were also writing code. It was simple code, but we were code writers nonetheless. Much like metal shop in the 1960s, when students learned skills suited to the industrial age, my friends and I were learning the skills of the digital age.

We sat in front of then space-age Apple II computers, trying the best we could to understand the concept of if/then computer code. Our assignment was to write our own code with the correct commands to send a document to the printer. When Rich Zimmerman got his code right and the huge dot-matrix printer started rumbling, it felt like we had just stepped into the future. (Funny enough, I still have days, thirty-five years later, when I feel a similar exuberance getting a wireless printer to work.)

While the details of code writing were foreign to my early

adolescent mind, the rules and structure were simple and logical. Here is an example of the kind of code we were writing back in Mr. Bancroft's class:

```
100 HOME
110 PRINT TAB(10); "APPLE WRITER TO PRINTER"
120 VTAB=5
130 INPUT"PATHNAME OF APPLE WRITER FILE PRINTED TO DISK: ";F$
140 IF F$="" THEN 900
145 VTAB=12
146 INPUT"CHARACTER TO REPLACE: ";X$
147 IF X$="" THEN 145[1]
```

It has a simple quality to it. "If X, then 145." Very reminiscent of many religious theologies and requirements: "If you do this . . . , then God will . . ."

For many people If/Then understanding is the presumed language of God. We have only heard that God tells us, "If you live this way, then I will bless you." "If you profess these convictions, then I will accept you." "If you pray, then I will listen." "If you turn away from sin, I will love you." The list goes on and on.

With its clear logical structure, I can see how that approach might feel safe, understandable, and doable. The beauty of computer tech classes in the 1980s was that they made something incredibly complex seem like something a teenager could do. If/Then rules create predictability and security.

That's also what the transactional approach to faith has going for it. If we can reduce our connection to God to an If/Then pattern, then we know what's expected of us and can set about doing it. But while the benefits of structuring computer code according to the rules are obvious, the results of If/Then requirements in human interaction and in our understanding of God are devastating.

Even if there were rules for connecting to God, the adapter would keep changing. There are regional variations, cultural shifts, changes in needs and expectations. The result is that there is no hope of ever truly being one with God under this system.

A Great Way to Doubt Yourself

The If/Then system can trigger a form of self-loathing. If God can't accept you as you are, then what are you supposed to do? How can you meet all the necessary requirements? As we grow and change, many of us are exhausted by our failure before God and our inability to adhere to a religious system. We only had to do what we were told, but it turns out we couldn't even muster the minimum required competency. So many people simply walk away.

In my early days of faith I would wonder what God might do in response to my wrongdoing. Would God punish me if I ran a stoplight or hurt someone? Would I face a future consequence for messing up? This can be a disorienting way to live, always wondering if we have met the requirements.

Just this morning I ran into a friend coming out of a store. She was recycling the aluminum pods from her espresso maker. I have the same machine and love it, so I asked why she was recycling the empty pods. "Do you trade them in for new ones?" I asked.

"No," she said.

"Oh, you're just doing your part to be a good global citizen," I quipped.

"I guess I am," she said, "for once. Maybe now I *will* get into heaven."

She was joking. She is not a religious person. But her comment reflected the expectation of people who really do feel the pressure of the If/Then system.

Another friend, Julie, was raised in a religious family. She put it like this: "For me and a number of my friends, we spent our entire lives running through a never-ending list of things we were supposed to do to be right with God. At some point we just swapped the 'If you . . .' for an 'F you' to the entire system. We want to be fully alive spiritual people. We realize that any system with preconditions, no matter how simple, is just the same song with a new tune. We don't want to dance to it any longer."

The transactional system, with its reliance on adapters and its emphasis on If/Then propositions, often leaves people with no other option but to turn their backs on the system. It can lead to dark places of emptiness and spiritual pain. In part, that's because the transactional system pulls the grace and freedom out of our relationship with God. It casts God in the role of all-powerful, never-satisfied King who constantly demands and demands and demands. In response, we have to keep changing adapters in an effort to stay relevant and necessary. We think it's worth the effort because if the next new adapter succeeds, it will satisfy the requirements. But in time we see that this is nothing more than a new round in the ever-shifting game of Jesus pleasing. It's a mess and people walk away.

Beneath these problems—the scarcity, the If/Then codes—is something far more problematic. If you'll continue to indulge my adapter analogy, it's as though the transactional system leaves God stuck inside a wall. The system relies on God being something Other, something distinct and set apart from us. According to that way of thinking, God is not here because God is over there. God is not near but far, not approachable but distant. It is as if God, too, is dependent upon the system.

If you have ever been separated from someone you love, say when traveling in another country, and you are trying to talk on the phone or by Skype but can't get the connection to hold, you know what it's like when both parties desperately want to connect but can't. This is similar to the If/Then system in faith. Both parties—you and God—are at the mercy of the system. And frankly that just seems silly.

The Greatness of God Does Not Require Separation

For many, there is a sense that the glory and wonder of God, as well as the majesty and holiness of God, require God to be separate from us. God is all those things, and we humans are none of those things. That means, according to this interpretation, that we require some sort of purification before we can engage with God. We're like a person in a HAZMAT suit leaving a toxic-waste site. We have to first go through a series of rooms to shed our protective gear and take a thorough shower to be rid of the toxins. Only then are we allowed to move out into the world.

For many of us, the required purification process for humans is something that honors God. But it seems to me that God doesn't need us to inflate the story in order to make God more grand. God accomplishes that without our help. There is nothing greater, more majestic, more grand than the God of all existence.

Jesus addressed this by calling for an end to the transactional system. When he taught using the "You have heard that it was said . . ." preamble, he often contrasted the truth he represented against a backdrop of the Old Testament's transactional system. His Jewish listeners were familiar with required sacrifices, prayers, dietary laws, purification rites, offerings, and more. But the story of God in Jesus is not one of swapping a set of adapters for the new, improved version. It's a story that the new way Jesus introduced *did away with* the need for adapters altogether.

The story of Jesus introduced an alternative to the transactional system. He did not present a slightly less stringent means of connecting with an Other God. Instead, he broke from the transactional system to put the story of God squarely in the life of humanity. The message of Jesus is that God connects directly with humanity. Jesus brought together God and humanity, which previously were assumed to be separate, irreversibly different, and completely unsuited pieces. We see this in his statement to his disciples: "On that day you will know that I am in my Father, you are in me, and I am in you."[2]

When we realize that we do not need a predetermined adapter in order to interact with God, we will live differently. When we give up trying to set just the right conditions to get God into us, we will approach God differently. We can begin to live in the reality that we are "In God," as Jesus and Paul put it.

When that happens, our understanding of God and of life changes. And when we have this new story in our heads—a life story and not a death story—it can make all the difference in how we live.

The integration of humanity and God was not a brand-new idea with Jesus. God's call always has been to live In God, not just to attempt to engage with God. The transactional approach has brought difficulty, destruction, and isolation to people and to all creation.

I like the way the apostle Paul wrote about this some two millennia ago: "I'm convinced that nothing can separate us from God's love in Christ Jesus our Lord: not death or life, not angels or rulers, not present things or future things, not powers or height or depth, or any other thing that is created."[3]

I like to think that Paul's "nothing" really means nothing. Not a thing. No adapters, connectors, or transactions are needed. We are all In God, right now.

And that can change everything.

Together from the Start

What If God's Requirements Are Nothing Like What We Thought?

[God desires] faithful love and not
sacrifice, the knowledge of God instead
of entirely burned offerings.

—Hosea, the prophet

My friend Claudio is a really smart guy who has a way with words. It's not just the words he chooses but also the way his mind works that is fascinating.

Claudio lives in Brazil and has spent a lot of time thinking about the way we humans live and interact with one another and the planet. He is part philosopher, part environmental activist, part urban farmer, part theologian. If you get him talking about the situation we find ourselves in with our planet, he will tell you that we don't have an environmental problem. Problems have fixes, he says. So what we have is a predicament, a great drama, really.

A drama calls for a response.

There is a big difference between fixes and responses. When we have a problem, we can use command-and-control approaches to fix it or change it or make it better. Stop, start, reset. When we're dealing with a drama, however, we have choices to make. In the midst of a drama, we are part of the situation. For Claudio it is clear that when it comes to the environment, we need a response, which involves choices. No one solution will fix things. Many responses will be necessary if we are to live well in this complex, wonderful world.

Understanding the difference between drama and problem has been helpful to me in many areas, including how to respond to one of the great dilemmas in the Bible. The dilemma involves repeated references to sacrifice.

Christianity and Judaism both have sacrifice stories, and it appears as if God is the one initiating the story. For Jews it is the call for Abraham to sacrifice his son Isaac. For Christians, it is the crucifixion of Jesus, God's Son.

How is it that we read so much about sacrifice (animal and otherwise) in the Bible, when Paul reminds us that God needs nothing from us:

God, who made the world and everything in it, is Lord of heaven and earth. He doesn't live in temples made with human hands. *Nor is God served by human hands, as though he needed something,* since he is the one who gives life, breath, and everything else. . . . In God we live, move, and exist.[1]

And from the prophet Hosea, writing some seven hundred years earlier:

I desire faithful love and not sacrifice,
  the knowledge of God instead of entirely
    burned offerings.[2]

And from Micah, another prophet:

Should I give my oldest child for my crime;
  the fruit of my body for the sin of my spirit?
He has told you, human one, what is good and
  what the Lord requires from you:
    to do justice, embrace faithful love, and
      walk humbly with your God.[3]

And from Jesus:

Go and learn what this means: "I want mercy and not
sacrifice."[4]

And even from the teachings of the early Jesus followers:

So, brothers and sisters, because of God's mercies, I encourage you to present your bodies as a living sacrifice that is holy and pleasing to God. This is your appropriate priestly service.[5]

So what is it? Does God demand a sacrifice, or is God looking instead for lives of mercy, justice, faithfulness, love, and humility? For many of us, the apparent switch from sacrifice to something better causes confusion. The drama comes to a head in the Abraham-Isaac story.

Abraham was ordered, it seems, to offer his son to God in the bloodiest way possible. Isaac, the son, was spared when a ram appeared in a nearby thicket. The ram was sacrificed instead. Later, prophets working for the same God rejected the very notion of sacrifice. And still later, it seems that another switch was introduced related to sacrifice. God had planned from before time to sacrifice Jesus as the Son of God.

This goes far beyond a Flip on God's part. It's more like a dizzying barrel roll.

There has to be a way for us to make sense of this. Is God the sacrifice-demanding God of the Old Testament, requiring blood sacrifice? Or is God the all-loving, grace-giving God of the New Testament? Many people have spent years going through the mental gymnastics required to make the clashing ideas of God somehow connect.

It is said that God's judgment *is* God's love, and that Jesus did away with the laws that bound God in the Old Testament. Coming from another perspective, it is said that the Old Testament stories are myths and the actions of God are all symbolic and representative. All of these perspectives, while offering some level of comfort, fail to take into account that we live In God. Being In God means there is no need to appease God or to get to God through sacrifice.

So how do we make sense of this call for sacrifice from God? For many, this is not simply a theological questions but an intensely personal dilemma.

What Kind of God . . . ?

"What kind of God is this that requires the death of a child?" my friend Brian asked with tears in his eyes. As a middle-aged man who had recently lost a child *and* a parent, he knew the unbearable pain of death. He wanted God to be the solution for death, or at least a comfort in the midst of it, not the one who demanded it.

Having been raised in a churchgoing family, Brian knew that Abraham was called to sacrifice Isaac, and it had always bothered him. "What kind of God is so starved for obedience or praise or to be worshiped that he would ask a man to plunge a knife into the chest of his own child?"

All I had to offer was a feeble response that went something like "Well, you know, Abraham didn't actually sacrifice Isaac in the end. God provided a ram that was sacrificed instead." My efforts didn't help.

"Oh, so this is a God who wants people to be *willing* to

sacrifice another human being in his honor! It is a God who pushes a father to his very breaking point and then says, 'Psych!' Somehow, that's even worse."

The thing is, I agree with Brian.

If the story of Abraham were told on television, it would fit the genre of dark character-driven shows only appropriate for HBO, cable, or Netflix. It has a certain Dexter quality to it, with the father of faith raising a knife to plunge it into his own flesh and blood.

The story of Abraham is central, of course, to the three major monotheistic faiths. That has not lessened the debate over what it means that Abraham took his son to a mountaintop, intending to put Isaac to death. I am not suggesting that I have the sole solution to a centuries-old problem. But as you might suspect, I made a Flip that allowed me to make sense of it. As it turns out, the key is found in the story itself.

Here is a brief classic-version recap.

Abraham was a righteous man. God promised Abraham and his wife, Sarah, that they would have a child. God also promised to be in a covenant relationship with all people through the child that God promised to the aging couple. God also promised to make Abraham the father of all nations.

The promised son, Isaac, was born, and some time later—tradition says when Isaac was in his teens—God broke the bad news to Abraham. As a test of Abraham's faith, he was to kill and burn his son on an altar as a sacrificial offering to God. Just as Abraham was about to go through with this gut-wrenching request, God called it off. God showed Abraham a ram caught in the brush. The ram was sacrificed in Isaac's place. At the last moment the boy was saved.

Told in a certain way the emphasis can be put on the faith of Abraham rather than the details of the test. The prospect of the ultimate act of violence, the dread experienced by the father and son as they made their way up the mountain to the altar, the revulsion that must have wracked Abraham as he anticipated plunging a knife into his son. It is far less troubling to be told about the test of faith. Preachers have reminded us that we, too, are tested. The story asks each of us, Are you willing to do what God asks? The answer depends on whether you or I have the faith of Abraham.

Framing the story this way allows us to avoid thinking about the legitimacy of God's giving a child, finally, to an elderly couple. And then God, when the promised son is twelve years old, telling the father to kill his son to prove the father's faith. And then putting a stop to it once the father carries out all the preparations and fulfills all the requirements, demonstrating his willingness to obey. Presenting the story as a test of faith helps us avoid the question of why anyone would want to follow such a cruel, sadistic God.

A Better Reading of the Abraham-Isaac Story

I think there is a better way to understand this story, a way that doesn't force us to avoid honest questions while still fitting the narrative of the bigger story of God. I want to suggest this is not a sacrifice story at all. It's a story about the Flip.

The Story of Us

The story of Abraham is not primarily about a man, his wife, and their child. Rather, it is a Bible story that plays out again and again in a kind of nonidentical repetition.

The story of Abraham is the story of everyone who has had to unpack assumptions, habits, and ideas that have been presented as required beliefs and practices. We are given such input by religion, culture, even our own imaginations. To accept that input without questioning it, however, can lead to a loss of faith.

The story is not about Abraham's faith being tested, but his willingness to take on a new faith. The story of Abraham is an archetype of the life of the people of Israel. The Jews moved from one story to another—from being bound to ancient stories to experiencing the Flip that God was gradually revealing. The inclusion of these stories in the Jewish Scriptures served as a model for how the nation of Israel was to transition. It showed them how they would live in the Promised Land as they moved from the culture, religion, and control of being enslaved in Egypt.

All good stories use structure as a method for helping readers (and listeners) understand them. When we read a book that starts "It was a dark and stormy night," we know our narrative genre. Likewise, when we watch a documentary, we do so with an expectation that it will tell a story from a certain perspective. When a movie opens with "The events depicted in this film took place in

Minnesota in 1987," we expect to see a real-life affair, even if the Coen brothers are making it all up.

The structure of Abraham's story suggests that it's more than a biography. It is meant to be read like a creation narrative with a larger, more universal truth being conveyed. The story is far more important than simply being the account of what happened to a man and his son one day as they carried a bundle of firewood and trudged up a mountain.

Abraham is meant to be seen as part of the creation narrative of the people of Israel. The narrative has to do with the creation of a people, the people of the god Yahweh. Think of these as family histories for an emerging faith. The stories answer the questions of who are we, how we got here, and how we should live.

The story of Abraham is the story of people being called from the religion of their land to the story of God.

Who Are We?

If you reread Genesis 11–12, you'll notice that Abraham is introduced with a backstory. His name first appears as Abram in a list of people descended from Noah. The lineage includes characters from Noah to Abraham and is filled with names and important events—floods, towers, wars. The fact that the larger narrative shifts suddenly from a major epic to a story about a specific individual sends a strong clue that Abram is an archetypal figure. He serves a far bigger purpose in the Genesis narrative.

Abram was one of three sons of Terah. In the midst of the

story, the narrative zooms in for a tight focus on Abram and his family.

> Terah took his son Abram, his grandson Lot (son of
> Haran), and his son Abram's wife, Sarai his daughter-in-
> law. They left Ur of the Chaldeans for the land of Canaan,
> and arriving at Haran, they settled there.[6]

What looks like a throwaway line—mentioning a location in passing—might be crucial to understanding what is being said. Abram was from Ur. Historians are fairly confident that Ur was in what is now called Iraq. There also is near-universal agreement on the religion of the Chaldeans (the King James Version refers to "Ur of the Chaldees"). Polytheistic Chaldeans believed in gods that demanded sacrifices of many kinds, including blood sacrifices.

When God got Abram's attention and told him to relocate, Abram was setting out from a land and a people where multiple gods were worshiped.

Another book of the Old Testament raises this issue along with a glimpse of the backstory:

> Then Joshua said to the entire people, "This is what the
> LORD, the God of Israel, says: Long ago your ancestors lived
> on the other side of the Euphrates. They served other gods.
> Among them was Terah the father of Abraham and Nahor.

I took Abraham your ancestor from the other side of the
Euphrates. I led him around through the whole land of
Canaan. I added to his descendants and gave him Isaac."[7]

We can assume that the gods of Abram's childhood were not
only familiar to him but were deeply rooted in his personal history. It is not unrealistic to assume that the gods still occupied a
place in his understanding of deity. Then the God of Israel told
him to leave Ur, leaving his tribal gods, to go to another place.
Abram was, in every way we can think of, changing direction.

It's easy to read a parallel story in the Hebrew Scriptures, with
the other story tracking the nation of Israel. The nation in the
time of Moses was called to leave Egypt and start over in a new
land. The trick for Abram and later for the enslaved Hebrews was
to leave behind their old story as they moved to a new place. Four
of the five books of the Torah describe how hard it was to let go of
the rituals of slavery. These included the culture of a foreign land
and an understanding of God that was embedded in the Hebrews, just as Abram had been influenced by the rituals and beliefs of Ur.

The LORD said to Abram, "Leave your land, your family,
and your father's household for the land that I will show
you. I will make of you a great nation and will bless you.
I will make your name respected, and you will be a
blessing."[8]

Then came Abram's name change. In his old age, he was given a new call, as if born anew with a new name at age ninety-nine. The new name marked a change of self-understanding from one life to another. The name change was part of a larger promise, that of a covenant between God and Abraham. The parallel is the covenant between God and the people of Israel.

> Abram fell on his face, and God said to him, "But me, my covenant is with you; you will be the ancestor of many nations. And because I have made you the ancestor of many nations, your name will no longer be Abram but Abraham. I will make you very fertile. I will produce nations from you, and kings will come from you. I will set up my covenant with you and your descendants after you in every generation as an enduring covenant. I will be your God and your descendants' God after you. I will give you and your descendants the land in which you are immigrants, the whole land of Canaan, as an enduring possession. And I will be their God."[9]

The name change, from Abram to Abraham, shifts the meaning of Abraham's life and identity. He had been "exalted father"; from now on he will be "the father of many."

From Abraham's renaming to the Isaac incident, this story is filled with hints that we should read it as an archetypal story of Israel. The people of Israel will move from the gods of Egypt to live in harmony with a covenant God. This is a coming-of-age story.

What's in a Name

But this is only part of what helped the story make sense for me. There are particularities of the names of God that became really important to understanding the story of Abraham.

The Jews had a bit of a dilemma. They were not to give God a name because God is ultimate reality and not simply a part of reality. Humans have no say over God. People could name animals and items and people, but not God. They were not to even try to speak the name of God, because God doesn't have a name. In the book of Exodus there is a famous story of Moses hearing the voice of God and asking what to call this voice. The response became a crucial tenant in Jewish faith, *ehyeh ašer ehyeh,* meaning "I Am Who I Am."[10] This conveys a combination of all existence, all that ever will be and all that is.

Jewish thought held that God was not a separate single subject to be named but rather the All of All. God is not simply in relationship with creation; God is the Essence and Sustainer of all creation. Even today you may see that some people will not write the word *God* but instead use *G-d.* This is an attempt to honor the tradition of not objectifying God with a name.

The Jews were not supposed to name God, but they had to refer to God in some way. And picking the right term for God is not easy. I don't like to use personal pronouns for God, such as *He* or *She,* because God is neither male nor female. But I don't want to refer to God as the gender-neutral *It.* So I use the term *God,* which at times makes for awkward sentences.

To avoid the problem of naming God, the Jews used descriptive titles for God. These included El Shaddai (Lord God Almighty), Adonai (Lord, Master), Jehovah Jireh (The Lord Will Provide), and others, including Yahweh (LORD). It is this last name that gets a lot of use in the Hebrew Bible—more than six thousand times in fact.

The title LORD, or Yahweh, is the word that was used in the story of Abram being called out of Ur and in the story of Abram being renamed Abraham. Also, at the announcement of a covenant with God, Abram fell facedown and the LORD (Yahweh) said to him . . .

A Director's Eye

At the risk of being too Sherlock-like (the recent BBC version, obviously), let me show you the subtle shift in the story that turns on the use of these titles or names. This is what helped me to see the sacrifice story as an un-sacrifice story. It is not a test of Abraham's faith but a test of willingness to listen to a new call. If we read the story as a television director might, something interesting happens.

The director's responsibility is to make the call on the mood and pacing of the lines delivered. The director gives input to actors about where to put the energy in the scene, and he or she makes sure the right person delivers the right lines.

Here is the text of the sacrifice narrative. See if you notice anything important.

After these events, God tested Abraham and said to him, "Abraham!"

Abraham answered, "I'm here."

God said, "Take your son, your only son whom you love, Isaac, and go to the land of Moriah. Offer him up as an entirely burned offering there on one of the mountains that I will show you."[11]

Did you see it? Perhaps not, because reading this in English we tend to see the word *God* as the generic word for deity. But because the story was written in Hebrew and a number of titles were used for God, the story becomes clearer when the titles for God are specified.

The term used for God in this story is the Hebrew word *Elohim*. "After these events, God (Elohim) tested Abraham . . ." That is a different word used for God's title. When Abram was called from his home to wander around, Yahweh called him. In English translations you will see *Yahweh* translated as "LORD" and *Elohim* translated as "God." Later, when Abraham is told to sacrifice the son he loves, Elohim gives the order.

The title *Elohim* is one of the terms used for God in the Old Testament, but it is not the only title used, and as it turns out, it was used as well in reference to Canaanite gods. The title *Elohim* is identical to the plural of *el,* and it means "gods" or "magistrates," a word also used for the pantheon of Canaanite gods.

In contrast, the passage that describes God's calling of Abraham names God as Yahweh (LORD). But there is a shift in the terminology used when Abraham is tested. Elohim told Abraham to take his son to the top of a mountain where he would sacrifice Isaac. This passage can be read as Elohim, "the many Canaanite gods," tested Abraham.

The use of the word *Elohim* grew in usage in the Jewish Bible amid hundreds of years of rabbinic debate. The debate centered on whether *Elohim* could comfortably be used for the Hebrew God without anyone mistaking it for the name of the ancient Canaanite gods. While it's not the case every time we see *Elohim* used in the Bible, I believe in this story we are meant to hear the ringing of ancient Canaanite gods testing Abraham. This fits with the archetypal story, a creation narrative that later would be reflected in the formation of the nation of Israel. The LORD (Yahweh) called the Hebrews out of Egypt, freeing them from slavery. At the same time, they were being called to The LORD (Yahweh) and away from the gods of Egypt.

This is where the television director comes in. The director would have to cast a voice for Elohim. When we hear the story acted out and spoken, and the role of Elohim is acted and spoken as Canaanite gods, we have a new kind of drama. We hear the gods of Abraham's childhood calling to him to return to the sacrificial story of his youth.

Back to the story of Abraham's test. Elohim said,

> Take your son, your only son whom you love, Isaac, and
> go to the land of Moriah. Offer him up as an entirely

burned offering there on one of the mountains that I will show you.[12]

Scholars differ on the meaning of ancient texts and words, and because of the nature of ancient languages, no one can say definitively what each word means. I am fairly confident that "land of Moriah" was meant to convey the land of the Amorites. In this we essentially hear the call of Elohim for Abraham to take his son to the place where human sacrifice was practiced. In other words, go back to the old place and the old story.

This way of hearing the story sets the nation of Israel in a great drama, a drama that resonates through the ages, one that many people can connect with. Abraham's story might be your story. It's the story of the man who wants to be faithful to his wife but is pulled by the loves of his previous life. It's the call of an addict who wants to maintain sobriety but feels the pressure of old patterns. It's the story of a person who wants to believe she is more than a culmination of her choices but feels trapped by her past.

It is the story of choosing what life we want to live: the one in front of us or the one behind. It is the story of the Flip, and in this instance it's a Flip to reaffirm a calling away from the old and into the new.

As the story moves to its climax, Abraham and the twelve-year-old Isaac make their way to the mountain.

They arrived at the place God [Elohim] had described to him. Abraham built an altar there and arranged the wood on it. He tied up his son Isaac and laid him on the altar on top of the wood. Then Abraham stretched out his hand and took the knife to kill his son as a sacrifice.[13]

Then comes the interruption, the halt, the shift, the Flip.

But the LORD's messenger called out to Abraham from heaven, "Abraham? Abraham?"

Abraham said, "I'm here."

The messenger said, "Don't stretch out your hand against the young man, and don't do anything to him."[14]

Did you see the change? The call to stop came from the messenger of Yahweh (the LORD).

If this were being produced as a television special, this second call would be spoken in a very different voice—the voice of Yahweh. This is the same voice that issued the promise to Abraham that he would be the ancestor of many, the one who offered the promise of life. The call for sacrifice came from Elohim, a title used for the gods of Abram's ancestry, while the call to stop the sacrifice came from Yahweh, the God of Abraham's future. The same God who made the covenant promise, the one who freed Israel from slavery. This great story shouts the truth that Yahweh is the God who stopped sacrifices.

I think we are supposed to hear that the LORD, Yahweh, the

Maker of this new covenant, does not desire sacrifice the way the religious systems of other nations do.

Elohim calls for sacrifice and Yahweh calls it off.

Flip.

Why the Back and Forth on Sacrifice?

Rather than thinking God swings back and forth, unsure about what God wants when it comes to sacrifice, we see the drama of different voices telling different stories. This is why Jesus could say "You have heard that it was said . . ." before turning the traditional understanding around. Plenty of voices were calling for maintaining the transactional system. Jesus would point to that before adding "But I say to you . . ." He called his followers to live into a different story.

The story always has included setting aside all forms of transactional religion, so a person no longer has to perform in strict accordance with the dictates of a god. Instead, we are to live, move, and exist In God.

This move away from sacrifice is a development not reserved only for the ancient Israelites. Throughout history there have been various types of sacrifice—animal, human, grain, and so forth—but that has changed dramatically. As a human race we have transitioned from the ways of life of our tribal ancestors. The development of human society is on the same trajectory as the story of Abraham, from tribalism and sacrifice to interconnection and life.

Human sacrifice is no longer acceptable anywhere in the world. Animal sacrifices are limited to rather obscure religious rituals, but they are not seen in mainstream religion. It is as if in religion, at least, we are starting to understand what Jesus proclaimed, that God desires mercy and not sacrifice.

Any time a system wants to use people as sacrificial fodder, we should reject it. The system can be religious, military, economic, or otherwise.

How we understand God's relationship to death and sacrifice has great influence over the way we live. Since people of Christian faith want to live harmoniously with God, it is easy to conclude that what is good for God is good for humanity. So if God is justified in demanding sacrifice, then we can justify sacrifice—even to the point of committing violence as a situational necessity. When God's justice or holiness is appeased by sacrifice, it makes transactional systems of faith not just an option but a requirement. You do this; God will do that. You perform the sacrifice; God will be satisfied. If you fail to adhere to the prescribed behavior, though, God will not listen to you.

Humanity can't live in a way of love, healing, and goodness when we understand the sacrifice of humans—even one—to be God's intention. Like Abram, we have a choice to hear the call to a better way of way of love and life, and this is what we see in Jesus. Which is where we turn next.

Reading Jesus Through
a Jesus-Flip Lens

How the Religious System Stacked the Deck and What We Can Do About It

> If you had known what this means, "I want
> mercy and not sacrifice," you wouldn't have
> condemned the innocent.
>
> —Jesus

"Jesus rose from the grave and you, you can't even get out of bed" was one of the song lyrics from the first Christian record album I ever owned.[1] Keith Green had a way of putting a point on his call for people to live for Jesus. Being new to the Christian faith when I heard this song, the sentiment rang true for me. I wanted to be as into God as God was into me. There was something good and right about that urge. But the power of the transactional religious system has a way of corrupting even the best of impulses.

Any argument that uses the "Hey, God did this for you; you really owe God a little something in return" is transactional. While seeming to be an honest calling for us to do our part, it actually is a threat to our life In God.

The quid-pro-quo understanding of God will lead us to missing the entirety of Jesus's message.

It is easy to convince ourselves there must be something we can do in response to the love of God. The forms of payback transactional faith come in calls to give up things that are precious to you: passions, time, family, career, and very often your money. I've never heard a preacher say, "With all that God has done for you, the least you can do is stay up late and enjoy some pizza and beer." Doing an enjoyable thing scores zero points on the religious-payback scale.

There certainly are times when we need to make changes in order to live well with one another, with God, and with the world. And this is where the story in your head makes a big difference. The story we live in shapes what we do and how we understand what we are doing. We tell ourselves a story, and we can tell ourselves a different, truer story. Changing the reason for what we do has as much power as changing our actions.

There are a number of healthy things we can do to live in a way that is more integrated with God. But it is possible for us to view those same actions as paying back God for God's love or doing the necessary things to reconnect with God. Instead, healthy practices should help us gain new perspective and, hopefully, lead to new outcomes.

I imagine you have had to walk in an area that has sketchy cellular coverage, starting and stopping, hoping to get one more bar of service. You know without thinking about it that this is not an instance of pacing excitedly because you're having an enjoyable conversation with the other person on the line.

Starting, stopping, going sideways, backing up, trying to get a better connection. Those actions are dictated by the system. We want to make a phone call, so we submit to the requirements (and whims) of the system.

How we approach connecting with God puts a lot of us in a similar situation. We can follow the established rules laid down by those who prop up the system. Or we can seek integration with God while rejecting the If/Then exchange.

We know this to be true in all our relationships. If we give a gift to someone because we thought of them and knew it would make their day, that is very different than if we give the gift in the hope that the person will now like us.

The Flip involves looking into your motivations. To show affection for someone because you love them is very different from showing affection in the hope you can talk to the person later about life insurance. The power of an action is not always in what we do but why. Eating a great meal to celebrate an accomplishment has a very different effect on your life than eating the same meal as a distraction from recent hurt or disappointment.

If you give money to ensure that Guatemalan orphans are loved and cared for because you want God to keep blessing you financially, you will remain trapped in a series of negotiations. You'll offer obedience in exchange for fewer obstacles in life, hoping God will agree to the deal. Being a person of moral conviction because you believe it will allow you to live wholly and honestly with others is a great calling. But living morally in an attempt to motivate God to answer your prayers is something entirely different.

You don't have to chase God or hurt for God or make a deal with God. God is not at all illusive. As Paul told the Athenians—and us—"God isn't far away from any of us."[2]

Your intention matters, the story in your head matters, and the story you are living matters.

Jesus Flips Religion

Jesus was heaven bent on discrediting systems that imposed performance requirements on a person who sought access to God. If you use the right words in prayer, God will hear you. If you obey the Law, God will think more highly of you. If you come to the specified place, you will find God. We read story after story of Jesus's showing how those who were outsiders to the religious system were not outsiders to God.

Religious systems can easily slip from being a benefit to humanity to asking humanity to serve the system. But God doesn't operate in that economy. God is the Giver, the Sustainer, the Essence of all. God invites us to participate, to build, to grow In God.

Telling this story was at the top of Jesus's agenda. He invited people to live freely and humanly as partners with one another and with God. Jesus was not offering a slimmed-down version of a rule-keeping faith. Instead, he issued a freeing invitation: "Come to me, all you who are struggling hard and carrying heavy loads, and I will give you rest. Put on my yoke, and learn from me. I'm gentle and humble. And you will find rest for yourselves. My yoke is easy to bear, and my burden is light."[3]

Sabbath Was More Than a Day Off Work

The end of the transactional system sounds great to anyone who has been oppressed by religious requirements. Still, Jesus had his work cut out for him getting this message out. The two big pinch points were the Sabbath and the temple. It is hard for twenty-first-century people to understand how heavily invested the first-century Jewish leaders were in these two religious institutions. In Jesus's day, people knew the dangers of challenging the temple system and presenting an alternative to strict adherence to rules regarding Sabbath observance.

At the time of Jesus you could not find a religious requirement with more clarity of significance and purpose than the Sabbath. The weekly day of rest and cessation from work was woven into the fabric of the Jewish faith. For many people of faith today, the Sabbath can seem like the most useful of the ancient If/Then requirements. A day of rest is just the thing many of us need. And the downside of the cessation of work on a Sunday is fairly insignificant, like the inability to shop for liquor (at least here in Minnesota), buy a car, or sink your teeth into a fresh Chick-fil-A sandwich.

But even the most Sabbath-concerned Christians don't get close to capturing the power and meaning of the Sabbath in the first century. The call to the Sabbath was a call to be like God, to do what God did. The Sabbath was not instituted by Moses at the time God gave him the Law. And it didn't come from Abraham the way the covenant and circumcision did. No, in the Hebrew story, the Sabbath was present at the beginning. We read about it in the Creation narrative:

> The heavens and the earth and all who live in them were completed. On the sixth day God completed all the work that he had done, and on the seventh day God rested from all the work that he had done. God blessed the seventh day and made it holy, because on it God rested from all the work of creation.[4]

God rested on the seventh day and so should humanity. It's a Godlike thing to do.

The Old Testament has hundreds of references to keeping the Sabbath, reinforcing the Creation story:

> Remember the Sabbath day and treat it as holy. Six days you may work and do all your tasks, but the seventh day is

a Sabbath to the LORD your God. Do not do any work on it—not you, your sons or daughters, your male or female servants, your animals, or the immigrant who is living with you. Because the LORD made the heavens and the earth, the sea, and everything that is in them in six days, but rested on the seventh day. That is why the LORD blessed the Sabbath day and made it holy.[5]

There is no way a first-century Jew could not know the importance of this, nor could he or she easily ignore the call to keep the Sabbath holy. Over the centuries, observance of the Sabbath became more complicated. For example, if you wanted to rest on the Sabbath, you had to define what constituted work. More accurately, the religious hierarchy defined for you what constituted work. The list became incredibly long and excruciatingly specific: no baking bread, no kneading bread, no tying things, no making of two loops in a rope, no lighting a fire, no extinguishing a fire, no carrying things farther than seven feet, and on and on.

To you, the list might seem petty, but those who tried to abide by these rules felt they were true attempts to keep the faith. That's one danger of the If/Then system. Someone has to set the rules and the rest of us are expected to adhere to them. Even the most wholehearted efforts to be faithful become limiting and restrictive rather than life giving and generative.

Then Jesus Flipped things. For one, he made a habit of healing people on the Sabbath. Last night at my church we read the story of Jesus's healing a blind man from John 9. The story includes an argument about whether Jesus was a prophet of God or a huckster. During a discussion at church, Skip asked, "Did Jesus ever heal anyone on any day other than the Sabbath?" The room broke into knowing laughter. While only about one-third of the reported healings happen on the Sabbath, you can't read the Gospels and not wonder if Jesus was going out of his way to make a point.

Jesus wanted those around him—and us as well—to Flip. The point of faith is not to keep rules regarding the Sabbath. The benefit to humanity is the point of faith. Jesus coined a phrase for this: "The Sabbath was created for humans; humans weren't created for the Sabbath."[6]

Jesus did not ask his followers to keep the Sabbath better; he called for a complete reorientation. The Sabbath should be followed if it benefitted humanity, but humanity was not to be burdened by Sabbath keeping in an attempt to impress God.

I believe Jesus's Flip on the Sabbath rule should guide all of our efforts, especially religious ones. We should commit to things that benefit humanity. We should never commit ourselves to things that build religion or seek to curry favor with God. Being faithful should bring wholeness.

It can seem odd to you and me that Jesus's Flipping the Sabbath turned into such a big issue. But his challenging the Sabbath and other religious rules and traditions, and by extension the authority of religious leaders, got Jesus killed.

Jesus returned to the synagogue. A man with a withered hand was there. Wanting to bring charges against Jesus, they were watching Jesus closely to see if he would heal on the Sabbath. He said to the man with the withered hand, "Step up where people can see you." Then he said to them, "Is it legal on the Sabbath to do good or to do evil, to save life or to kill?" But they said nothing. Looking around at them with anger, deeply grieved at their unyielding hearts, he said to the man, "Stretch out your hand." So he did, and his hand was made healthy. At that, the Pharisees got together with the supporters of Herod to plan how to destroy Jesus.[7]

Jesus wasn't just making a little adjustment; he was Flipping the system on its head. Those who stood the most to lose worried that if he could enlist enough support and attract enough followers, it could put the entire system in jeopardy.

The Temple Was at the Center of It All

The gospel of John gives a bit of insight into why the religious leaders were so worried about Jesus. His way of teaching was attractive to people who were often on the outside of the religious system, people who had no vested interest in propping up the transactional system. If enough followers of Jesus started wielding influence and the movement grew, it would bring an end to the temple structure, and that would have national consequences.

Then the chief priests and Pharisees called together the council and said, "What are we going to do? This man is doing many miraculous signs! If we let him go on like this, everyone will believe in him. Then the Romans will come and take away both our temple and our people."[8]

The rules of temple worship and animal sacrifice were presented as the backbone not just of Judaism but also as the strength of Israel's identity as a nation. The center of Jewish faith was the temple. It is nearly impossible to overstate the importance and power of the temple in people's religious and civic lives and in their ideas about God, humanity, and the fate of the world. The temple was thought not only to be the center of the life of God but also a blessing to every person in the world. Many considered it to be the center of God's activity in the world.

There had been two iterations of the temple in Jerusalem. The first was built by Solomon in roughly 950 BCE. When that temple was destroyed by the Babylonians four hundred years later, there was great worry that the nation of Israel would lose its identity. The temple was rebuilt in the 500s BCE, and the nation worried for generations that it would be destroyed again.

The temple sat in the center of Jerusalem both figuratively and literally. It was part civic-gathering place and part sacrificial center. The function of sacrifice in the Jewish religion is complex. While it is clear that there was an entire temple dedicated to the practice of animal sacrifice, for centuries the prophets were calling the nation away from sacrifice to prayer. In 725 BCE, Hosea called the nation to "prepare to speak and return to the LORD; say to the LORD, 'Forgive all wickedness; and receive the good. Instead of bulls, let us offer what we can say.'"[9]

This evolving Jewish faith and call for changing temple practice moved in and out of vogue over the centuries as the influence of the priests and the prophets ebbed and flowed. It is clear that the prophets' call for change was popular with Jesus and his followers.

The sacrificial system of the temple stands as a direct challenge to the call of God. Any transactional system involves cumbersome and often contradictory rules. The rules frustrate even those who try hardest to comply. Jesus went out of his way to point out the limitations of such a system.

Spirit and Truth, Not Sabbath and Temple

In Jesus's time there were Roman, Greek, Egyptian, and other versions of religion and spirituality. Even within the Hebrews' religious tradition there were layers and differing versions. In Jesus's time, conflicts and disagreements existed among Pharisees, Sadducees, teachers of the Law, Herodians, Zealots, and others. Then there were groups that were excluded, such as Samaritans, who were part Jewish and part Assyrian. A seven-hundred-year-old ethnic divide kept all Samaritans out of the temple. They proclaimed they were right in worshiping God on a mountain in their own territory. As we see today, there was a great deal of disagreement over who was practicing the right version of the faith.

Jesus made use of an encounter with a Samaritan woman to introduce a Flip. At first she dismissed him, but then she realized Jesus was a special teacher of the way of God. She said, "I see that you are a prophet. Our ancestors worshipped on this mountain, but you and your people say that it is necessary to worship in Jerusalem."[10]

Here was a situation ripe for Jesus to bring out the Flip. He rejected the divide between Jews and Samaritans. Instead, he called for the Samaritan woman to live in a new reality.

> Believe me, woman, the time is coming when you and
> your people will worship the Father neither on this
> mountain nor in Jerusalem. You and your people worship
> what you don't know; we worship what we know because
> salvation is from the Jews. But the time is coming—and is
> here!—when true worshippers will worship in spirit and
> truth. The Father looks for those who worship him this
> way. God is spirit, and it is necessary to worship God in
> spirit and truth.[11]

There is no limit to God or where you can find God. The time is now to believe that God is Spirit and not a building or a location on a prescribed mountain. All are invited to live harmoniously with God in spirit and truth and to do this in all sorts of unspecified places.

It is difficult, some two millennia later, to understand the complicated history involving the temple and its practices. But we know that Jesus opposed the temple's serving itself and using people for its own survival. Jesus famously entered the temple courts and ran out the money exchangers, saying, "My house will be called a house of prayer for all nations. . . . But you've turned it into a hideout for crooks."[12]

Jesus wasn't talking about commerce; he was talking about robbery. He was angry at the dishonest practices of the money changers, which not only robbed people of money but also robbed their souls by erecting a barrier to what many perceived as access to God. The fraudulent money exchange exemplified the way the temple system had become a transaction that required people to pay for what they were told was access to God. The system was so corrupt that it no longer served any benefit to the people's lives.

Two Pennies for a New Thought

The temple was not only a place where money could be exchanged for travelers from other regions but also where animals could be purchased for temple-approved sacrifices. Money also changed hands in the form of weekly offerings. A big operation such as the temple, or any other religious system, requires a steady influx of cash. It takes a high volume of human and financial resources to maintain a transactional relationship between God and humanity.

This brings us to Jesus's comments about the widow who came to give her offering at the temple. She contributed two copper coins, and like a lot of pastors, I had misheard and misinterpreted this story. I have told people to be like this woman, to see her as an exemplary model of faith. Turns out I had missed the point.

When I first heard the story, I was influenced by the idea that we should give ourselves for God's benefit. I had not yet been exposed to the idea that our life In God is for the benefit of humanity. And without knowing it, I read only part of the story. Here is the full story as recorded in the gospel of Mark:

Jesus sat across from the collection box for the temple treasury and observed how the crowd gave their money. Many rich people were throwing in lots of money. One poor widow came forward and put in two small copper coins worth a penny. Jesus called his disciples to him and said, "I assure you that this poor widow has put in more than everyone who's been putting money in the treasury. All of them are giving out of their spare change. But she from her hopeless poverty has given everything she had, even what she needed to live on."[13]

Picture the scene: Jesus and his disciples are watching the happenings around the temple, which wasn't just one building but a complex of buildings and public spaces. And old woman, long widowed, makes her way into the public area. Rich people are putting large amounts of money into the collection cisterns. The old woman reaches into her pouch and removes two copper coins. Somehow Jesus notices this and concludes that it is all the money she has. She gives away the money she needs to live on.

Jesus points the woman out to his disciples, and this is where my initial reading went wrong.

I thought Jesus was saying the woman did something admirable, something he wanted the disciples to emulate. She was humble and didn't make a big deal of her sacrificial contribution. Unlike the rich people around her, she could trust God for everything and hold nothing back. I thought Jesus was saying, "See this woman? She is your example of full submission to God."

But there is nothing in the text that indicates any of that. I had read that *into* the story.

Once a version of a story gets into my head, it doesn't leave without first putting up a fight. I used this story when I spoke at youth retreats. The typical rhythm would include a time on Saturday night for the teenagers to contemplate their faith and make a decision about how they wanted to live. After two or three talks over a twenty-four-hour period, my role was to use the Saturday-night talk to bring the students to a place where they could set aside things in their lives that were keeping them from God.

A key to being an effective Saturday-night closer (one who could get all or most of the kids to make a public declaration of a new faith or a better way to live their faith) was to tell a series of compelling stories and issue a clear call to action. My understanding of the story of the widow with the two coins was perfect for this. The ask was clear: "Is there anything you are keeping from God that you need to sacrifice for the sake of your faith? Will you be like the widow and give to God all that you need to live on?"

I structured the talk for maximum visceral connection. When each person came into the room, he or she was given two pennies. In the center aisle at the front of the room was a big metal bowl, the kind of bowl that would resound with the sound of commitment when a penny landed in it.

I would talk about people with great faith who had sacrificed much and had seen great things from their faith. I would tell the story of the widow with impassioned detail. I wanted the teenagers to picture this old woman with her two coins. I challenged them not to wait until they were too old to do what Jesus was asking of them. I urged them to give God all they had to live on right then and there. I asked them to let the coins in their hands represent all they were holding on to—sports, relationships, the future, their reputations, their pain—and to walk forward as the widow did. I urged them to drop the pennies into the bowl.

And they did. Every time I used this talk, accompanied by the sniffling of teenagers, the room would fill with the sound of the coins hitting the bowl. On Sunday morning I would suggest that any time they received two pennies as change, they could leave them in the penny jar at the cash register. It could be an act of recommitment.

I now have mixed emotions about such tactics. I know for many students this was a sincere expression of living a healthy life with God. And I was sincere in my efforts to help them live that way. But I also know that for others it was an exercise in playing an expected role in a pressured system of If/Then transactions. If you give your all, if you stand in front of your peers and drop your pennies into the metal bowl, God will take notice and you will experience God's presence.

I'm not sure many of the students ever thought of it again, but I know I did.

And then, about a year ago, I Flipped on the story of the widow who gave all she had. At my church, Solomon's Porch, we use an open discussion group on Tuesdays to put together the sermon for the following Sunday. We were reading this story, and I was telling the group how I had used it at retreats. A man who was visiting had joined us for the evening. When I finished talking, he said, "I think you have that story totally wrong." As he explained himself, I knew he was right.

He suggested that Jesus wasn't using this woman as an exemplar of the faith. Instead, Jesus was pointing her out as a victim of the temple's requirements. Jesus wasn't saying, "Be like this woman." He was saying, "Be careful or you will be like this woman. This system will leave you penniless and broke. It will take all you've got and leave you with nothing to live on." It was as if he were saying, "For the rich this system works fine. But for those who have given all they have, they end up with nothing."

This guy pointed out the verses that preceded this story. Jesus was in the temple issuing warnings: "Watch out for the legal experts. They like to walk around in long robes. They want to be greeted with honor in the markets. They long for places of honor in the synagogues and at banquets. They are the ones who cheat widows out of their homes, and to show off they say long prayers."[14]

Then a widow came along and proved Jesus's point. The rest of the story solidified for me this new—or rather, old—understanding of what Jesus was saying. Here it is.

> As Jesus left the temple, one of his disciples said to him, "Teacher, look! What awesome stones and buildings!"
>
> Jesus responded, "Do you see these enormous buildings? Not even one stone will be left upon another. All will be demolished."[15]

Jesus was saying this entire system, not just the structure of this magnificent temple, would not stand.

The System's End and Life's New Start

It is ironic that we so easily slip into seeing the grandeur and beauty of powerful systems and miss the point that exploitative religious systems are not what the life of God will produce. This gives real power to Jesus's reminding his disciples to avoid thinking of the destruction of the temple as the end of the life of God. It never was the life of God.

> Jesus answered, "Destroy this temple and in three days I'll raise it up."
>
> The Jewish leaders replied, "It took forty-six years to

build this temple, and you will raise it up in three days?"
But the temple Jesus was talking about was his body.[16]

We hear the same thing when the apostle Paul calls others to see their bodies as temples: "Don't you know that your body is a temple of the Holy Spirit who is in you?"[17]

What a Flip.

My wife is a yoga instructor who finds many parallels to the teaching of Jesus in her yoga practice. Her instructor, Ganga White, wrote a poem that is famous in the yoga world. I think it resonates with Jesus's engagement with the Samaritan woman on the mountain, his empathy with the widow, and his call for us to find the life of God in all places.

What If?

What if our religion was each other?
If our practice was our life?
If prayer was our words?
What if the Temple was the Earth?
If forests were our church?
If holy water—the rivers, lakes and oceans?
What if meditation was our relationships?
If the Teacher was life?
If wisdom was self-knowledge?
If love was the center of our being[18]

It sounds a lot like Jesus's saying that the blessed are not the temples and building, the blessed are not the special people who are granted access to special places and practices, but

> Blessed are the poor in spirit,
>> for theirs is the kingdom of heaven.
> Blessed are those who mourn,
>> for they will be comforted.
> Blessed are the meek,
>> for they will inherit the earth.
> Blessed are those who hunger and thirst for
>>> righteousness,
>> for they will be filled.
> Blessed are the merciful,
>> for they will be shown mercy.
> Blessed are the pure in heart,
>> for they will see God.
> Blessed are the peacemakers,
>> for they will be called children of God.
> Blessed are those who are persecuted because of
>>> righteousness,
>> for theirs is the kingdom of heaven.

Blessed are you when people insult you, persecute you and falsely say all kinds of evil against you because of me.[19]

These familiar but neglected words of Jesus sound a lot like the results when we understand that In God we live, move, and exist.

So let's talk about what it means be In God and how that opens new opportunities for healing the human spirit, fostering life in community, and living responsibly with God, with one another, and with the earth.

Love Is Never the Wrong Way

The One Reliable Guide for All Flips

Love your enemies and pray
for those who harass you.

—Jesus

I had only been a Christian a short time when I ran across a disturbing statement in my Bible. It was printed in red letters, which meant it came from Jesus, which meant I couldn't dismiss it as easily as I initially wanted to.

"Be perfect . . . as your heavenly Father is perfect."[1]

Boy, did that seem to step up what was required of a person. Perfection, really?

Like any right-minded person I knew it was impossible to be perfect, to never make a mistake, to somehow be like God. But since Jesus said it, I wanted to take it seriously.

I was new to the faith, so I figured he must have been using hyperbole, because no Christians I knew had even gotten close to perfection. But the consistent lack of achievement in this area didn't stop the faithful from calling for perfection, even though it was referred to as sanctification or justification or righteousness.

The tribe of Christians I was part of at the start of my Christian journey were kind, others-focused evangelicals who wanted faith to be life giving. So they avoided pushing the "be perfect" idea too directly.

But once I was sensitive to the call to perfection, it seemed I was seeing it everywhere in the Bible. Paul and King Solomon got into the act: "I'm sure about this: the one who started a good work in you will stay with you to complete the job by the day of Christ Jesus." "Train children in the way they should go; when they grow old, they won't depart from it." "It's not that I have already reached this goal or have already been perfected, but I pursue it, so that I may grab hold of it because Christ grabbed hold of me for just this purpose."[2] It went on and on.

I plucked these passages and others out of context and wove them together into an endless call for unblemished righteousness. I wanted to follow Jesus, and as far as I knew, this was the way to do it. Perfection, here I come.

I eventually was Flipped on my understanding of this call for perfection. But it didn't happen until I became keenly aware of the power of the never-achievable, perfection-seeking rabbit hole that chips away at a person's spirit. Having an unreachable goal for life is exhausting and relationally toxic.

The only sense I could make out of biblical calls for personal holiness, righteousness, or perfection was that my life would require constant vigilance in word, thought, and deed. I was trying to live up to what I saw as my calling from Jesus. This impulse is still my motivation in much of my life, but after the Flip, I understand it differently.

When I was younger I worked hard to keep my body pure. I was a high school and college athlete, so I understood what it meant to make physical sacrifices in the name of a higher goal. And while I wasn't much of a student, I knew that people who studied and worked hard made better grades than I did. So I saw studying my Bible every day, talking about it every day, and working at making sense of what God was saying to me through the Bible as keys to really understanding my faith. I stopped swearing because Jesus said, "It's not what goes into the mouth that contaminates a person in God's sight. It's what comes out of the mouth that contaminates the person."[3]

I got from that verse that I should not be a potty mouth. I even gave my girlfriend a little lecture when an "Oh, shit" came from her mouth after a near car accident. "You know," I said, in that tone that can come only from someone who takes perfection seriously and wishes other people would too, "you might want to check your heart and see why it was those words you turned to in a time a need."

I mean seriously. I don't know how she's stayed with me all these years.

We All Want to Grow

What makes it hard to dismiss all this moral-perfection seeking as being utterly misguided is that we all want to grow, to be better, to be freed from experiences and beliefs and ideas about life that have us trapped. We *want* to leave behind old patterns that hold us back. We want to lean into a full life. We want to pursue something like perfection. At least that is what I wanted.

But here's what I've come to believe: those desires are not what is expressed in pursuits of moralistic perfection or the skewed version of spiritual righteousness I learned from an If/Then theology.

The crucial impulses of wanting to grow, to get smarter and be kinder and better, come from maturing and becoming aware of how we can and should live in the world. They all have to do with living, moving, and existing In God.

Instead of being part of some transaction in which we have to do X and Y to become who God wants us to be, we already are In God, gloriously ever connected with God and one another. All of us, with our abilities, limits, wounds, passions, and goodness wrapped in struggle, failure, and angst. We don't need an upgrade in order to be free of what traps us.

We need the freeing power of uncontrollable, unbound love—the love that is In God. It is love that sets us free. And we are set free to love. As it turns out, that is what Jesus was getting at all along with his "be perfect" call. While I saw perfection as a moral calling, Jesus was saying "be perfect in your love."

Trusting in Love

One of my college professors explained, "When Jesus said 'Be perfect as your heavenly Father is perfect,' he was saying 'Just as God is perfect in loving all people, so are you to be perfect in loving all people.'"

Flip.

Be made perfect in love, by love, through love. Not training for a spiritual race, not killing the old self, not judging the good and bad. Loving, pure and simple. I admit that while that sounded good, it didn't sound right. Not until I read the passage in Matthew a few more times.

While I had memorized the "be perfect" line as a standalone verse, Matthew 5:48 is actually the culminating line of a longer quote. And that longer quote changed my understanding of the last line completely:

> You have heard that it was said, "Love your neighbor and
> hate your enemy." But I tell you, love your enemies and
> pray for those who persecute you, that you may be children
> of your Father in heaven. He causes his sun to rise on the
> evil and the good, and sends rain on the righteous and the
> unrighteous. If you love those who love you, what reward
> will you get? Are not even the tax collectors doing that?

And if you greet only your own people, what are you doing more than others? Do not even pagans do that? Be perfect, therefore, as your heavenly Father is perfect.[4]

There Ain't No Good Guys; There Ain't No Bad Guys

This is one of Jesus's classic Flips. "You have heard that it was said. . . . But I say to you . . ." In Jesus's day, not unlike today, there was much debate about who counted as a neighbor. If a person qualified, then Jesus's followers would feel okay about loving that person.

But Jesus told them to Flip. He said not to simply follow the cultural customs of separating people based on how close or far away they live, or by who is like you and who isn't. Rather, be like God who loves all of them. Love everyone the way God loves everyone.

This wasn't an easy message for people to hear. The first century was filled with serious dangers for the Jewish community, living in occupied territory under Roman rule. The Jews' history was filled with exile, deportation, and occupation. When Jesus walked the earth, the temple in Jerusalem had been destroyed once in the past and would be destroyed again a few decades later, in 70 CE. Their fears of suffering even greater destruction at the hands of Rome's legions were real. The Jews had good reason to fear that Israel would cease to exist and the people would once again be dispersed among gentiles far from the land God had given them. So loving your enemy carried powerful consequences.

Jesus was not saying "Stop believing you have enemies." He was saying "Yes, your enemies are real, and here is a better way to approach your enemies: with the same love you have for a friend." He wanted to Flip the old system of repaying hate with hate, pitting enemy against enemy.

But when you feel your nation, your friends, and your family are besieged or at war, you tend to feel justified in drawing clear lines between friend and enemy. I felt this tension in the days following the attacks of September 11, 2001. I had both a deep sense of patriotism and connection with my fellow citizens, but I also had the sickening feeling that I didn't know who to trust. I really wanted clarity on who were the good guys and who were the bad guys. The easiest place to start looking for enemies was among those I knew least or who seemed the least like me. During that time it was hard to hear Jesus saying I shouldn't be putting people into good-guys and bad-guys categories.

Overcoming Our Impulses

Overcoming these impulses is no easy task. The human capacity to recognize a person as stranger and suspect, and another person as safe and trustworthy, is built into our brains. A normally developing infant begins to recognize faces at about three months. It's a great stage when babies start lighting up at the sight of their parents. They smile for anyone they recognize. But at the age of six months or so, the brain develops the ability to make judgments about faces and responds differently to people who are unfamiliar. This is when stranger anxiety can set in, making even the friendliest baby temporarily wary even of people who've known her since birth.

I'm part of a church with lots of new babies, and many of us love to help out new parents by holding their babies. It's not uncommon to see a person reach for a six-month-old only to be met with the "I don't know you" cry. Knowing this is a normal developmental stage can help everyone involved—well, maybe not the baby—feel better about this alarming response to kindness.

Unfortunately, vestiges of stranger anxiety remain in us as adults. The shrieking and crying of our infant days is replaced by coldness, silence, or indifference toward anyone we consider a stranger. Most of us find it more natural to connect with people who sound and act the way we do, so we tend to cluster with those who are familiar. If we end up interacting with people different from us, in our minds we consider them a kind of stranger. We trust someone who reminds us of our own family and distrust or fear those who are noticeably different.

This differentiation happens in all societies and comes about in formal and subtle ways. Humans differentiate along lines of ethnicity and race. In Africa, it is common to see isolation based on a person's tribal clan. In India, it comes in the form of the caste system. In China, important distinctions are made between city people and rural people. Wherever indigenous peoples have shared their land with others, the indigenous population has become the marginalized population. And nearly everywhere in the world, distinctions are made based on wealth.

My friend Shane Claiborne likes to remind us, "Our problem is not that we don't love the poor; our problem is that we don't know the poor." We need to address the subtle fear we feel toward the other, no matter where it appears. Jesus calls us to grow, to develop, to move beyond our simple biological impulses and be like God in our love of others.

The call of our faith is to help us move beyond inborn tribal impulses.

Love Has No Contingencies

We are called to replace the consequences of judgment with love. Just as God does not judge but "causes his sun to rise on the evil and the good, and sends rain on the righteous and the unrighteous."[5] Here is the Flip. We need to resist making love contingent on anything. If God is not choosy, then why would we need to be? This is why Jesus tells us to be like God, to love everyone. No matter what.

My friend Kati shares great quotes from others on her Facebook wall. I love seeing her posts. The other day she posted one: "There isn't a person in the world you wouldn't love if you could read their story."

What makes someone appear unlovable often is the simple fact that we don't know the person. The beautiful implication of living, moving, and existing In God is that we are fully known by God and fully loved by God. God needs no filter to see us as lovable. While there are versions of the faith that want us to believe we are not suitable to be in the presence of God, Jesus tells us to love one another as God loves us, without judgment. The story of God is that we are loved by God fully, completely, with no required upgrade. And we are called to love the way God loves, not holding back our rain or sun from anyone.

Jesus often connects the way we live with one another to the way we live with God, as if there is no difference between the two. When you love one another, you love like God. When you curse your brother, you curse God. When you don't forgive, you are not forgiven. In God we all are integrated. There's no pulling one part away from the other. Love is not the reward; it is the norm, the constant. It is the way of God, the perfect way.

All this loving and accepting without consideration of the righteousness or unrighteousness of the other person—or of ourselves—can be unnerving. Everyone wants God to be forgiving but only when the conditions are met. That fits the transactional system, and somehow it seems right. It's only fair that a person in need of forgiveness do something to merit being forgiven.

But transactional thinking often takes us even farther afield. It is natural to think that those who have done really horrible things are beyond God's love. They chose to act in terrible ways against people and against God, so they deserve what they're about to get. The truth is they aren't beyond God's love.

Another form taken by If/Then thinking is that without the threat of losing God's love, people won't be motivated to grow and be better. Why would anyone be driven to improve if there were not the very real possibility of losing favor in God's eyes? This type of transactional view feels right, in part, because it's consistent with an incentive-based market economy. If we don't give people a sufficient financial incentive to work hard, they will just be lazy. Likewise, if we don't scare people into living right, they'll thumb their noses at God.

Not only is that rarely the case in economics (as most people work hard and do the right thing for many other and better reasons beyond money), but when it comes to a life change, love is not the reward but the initiator. The apostle Paul made this point in a letter to the Christians living in Rome who were trapped in judgment of one another. He wanted them to replace judgment with love. He wrote, "Do you have contempt for the riches of God's generosity, tolerance, and patience? Don't you realize that God's kindness is supposed to lead you to change your heart and life?"[6]

Living, moving, and existing In God eliminates the in-or-out dichotomy, the good-or-bad value judgments. It does away with the need for a performance-based life. We must return hate with love. We must combat death with life. This is what we see in Jesus, who was the victim of great hate and murderous threats—threats that motivated action and ended with his execution. So when Jesus called us to love our enemies, the idea was not coming from a high-minded ethical or spiritual-only impulse. It was coming from an awareness that his enemies would inflict their hate on him and bring about his death. "Love your enemy" was not an inspirational longing; it was the essence of Jesus's life.

This call to love everyone raises many real-world problems. Life is full of people doing really bad things to one another. How are we to respond? It is easy to think that love is no match for evil. Love can seem so soft, so forgiving, so dismissive of the harm brought about by evil. To be honest, there is a part of me that would prefer to reserve love for those who deserve it, to counteract violence and hate with more of the same. It's easy to believe that the If/Then nature of the world really does require us to not be too free with love.

Love over Wrongdoing

I'm sure you have encountered the perspective that says if we give love to the wrong people, or to people who do the wrong things, then we are making light of wrongdoing. According to this line of thinking, it's not loving to let other people live in ways that could be considered sinful. It's like a track meet in elementary school where every kid who entered a race gets a medal. Real athletes know that if everyone gets a reward, then no one does.

But the love of God doesn't work like that. I was in college when I was first confronted with the most radical version of God's love. One of my professors told us he was going to prison to visit an inmate. This was not just any inmate; it was a person who had harmed the professor's daughter. My professor was going to show care for a person who had caused so much pain to his daughter and his wife and him. I wondered out loud in class why he thought this man deserved his forgiveness and love. I asked, "Did this guy ask for your daughter's forgiveness?"

What I really wanted to know was whether the inmate deserved the love and grace my professor was showing him. But he didn't answer my question. Instead, he said that in doing this over the last few years, he was pretty sure he had brought something good to the perpetrator. And he knew for sure that visiting the man who had caused him and his family so much pain had brought healing to his heart and to his daughter. He knew that there was a limit to how much he could hate. He had gone all the way down that hole, and it left him angry and damaged.

He told us that he'd thought about all the vengeful things he wanted to do to this man, how he burned with a need for revenge. And he told us how empty and wounded those feelings had left him. Now he wanted to see if he could love his enemy.

I was so struck by this story as a college student. Now, some thirty years later, I still long for the confidence that I would do the same thing. I want to love my enemy, but frankly, most days, it's all I can do to love those who love me.

I want to grow in giving the kind of love that is undeserved. I have recently come to the conclusion that violence is the opposite of love, regardless of the reason for it. I have rather reluctantly become committed to nonviolence. I have found it helpful to consider any ways in which I participate in violence, and I do what I can to remove those things from my life. As part of cultivating a life of nonviolence, I make every possible effort to not intentionally kill any living creature.

I should be clear: I eat meat, and I am fully willing to allow other people to do the work of providing my food for me. Like I said, I'm still working on it. I know it is a bit over the top to scoop up a spider and carry it outside or to shoo away a mosquito, but I do it as a way to try and inflict no harm. This is helping me recognize how easily I have defaulted to the use of death. I don't begrudge people who swat a bug or use a mouse trap or catch a fish, and I'm not doing this because I think it makes me a superior person. Instead, I am committed to finding other ways to use my body in line with Jesus's ethic of life and not my own default setting of destruction.

If you grew up in the United States, the last remaining world superpower, you know the assumption is that military force is the only realistic solution to just about any perceived international threat. I am convinced that our reliance on military solutions breeds a cycle of violence. I hear both personal and global implications in Jesus's warning: "All those who use the sword will die by the sword."[7]

It has become clear to me that the only way military violence makes sense is to declare some people as innocent and others as not. This seems to go against Jesus's call to perfect love.

A newspaper headline on a newsstand fifteen feet from me reads, "Innocent American Beheaded in Syria." The article tells of the beheading of a second journalist by the group known as ISIS.

This horrible, profoundly disturbing story was followed up by a story about US drones blowing up a caravan in Somalia and killing the mastermind of terror attacks in that nation. The story of the deaths of two Western journalists was framed as a tragedy, and the air assault in Somalia was framed as an accomplishment. This only makes sense if we accept that there are two distinct categories of people: one group acceptable and the other irredeemably not acceptable. This is the type of thinking that Jesus called us to reject.

Love, Not Violence

The second conflict I have—and I believe followers of Jesus should all have—is the ease with which we commingle a wrong understanding of God's love with acts of violence and death. In 2010 I participated in the Seeds of Compassion event in Seattle, organized around the visit of the Dalai Lama. As one of the presenters, I took part in a small gathering with the Dalai Lama and South African bishop Desmond Tutu.

These two men have committed their lives to peace and nonviolence. Their work has saved countless lives and made the world a safer place. They both are committed to the call to love their enemies just as they would love their friends. They have lived out this commitment in ways that most of us can't imagine. For both men, this commitment stems from a deep faith in the presence of the divine in all people.

I heard Bishop Tutu say, "If we truly understood that God is fully present in all, we would be compelled to genuflect even upon meeting a stranger."

These are legendary men of peace, love, and nonviolence. They have a great rapport with each other. Sitting just ten feet from them, I saw how they lovingly tease each other, smile almost constantly, can hardly finish a sentence without laughter. They are really fun to watch. I'm not sure why I noticed their feet, but seeing the Dalai Lama wearing Velcro-strapped tennis shoes under his robe kept me from being totally overwhelmed by the presence of these great men.

I had noticed the Dalai Lama's entourage when he entered the room. He was surrounded by twenty or so large monks dressed in bright-orange kasaya robes. Surprisingly, they were bigger than I would have expected Tibetans to be. They walked with purpose, creating a clear path in front of and on all sides of his holiness. Their entrance was quite a spectacle.

As the spiritual leader of the Tibetan people, the Dalai Lama is treated with the same regard as a head of state on a diplomatic visit to the United States. So in addition to his rather large, young, fit monk friends, there was a pack of Secret Service agents around him. Like the monks, they had their own distinct look: dark suits, inconspicuous earpieces, and that bulk around their chests caused by Kevlar vests.

They stood at the ready with one hand firmly in control of their Sig Sauer P229 handguns under their jackets. While I did not see it clearly, I'm pretty sure one agent also was in possession of an MP5 submachine gun. To put it mildly, they were not only a protective force, they were a well-trained lethal force.

The world is a complicated place. Here were two men who have done as much as anyone to advocate on behalf of peace, not only in Tibet and South Africa but in the global consciousness. They have talked about it, written about it, and demonstrated it in their own lives. They are without argument men of peace, but they were protected by lethal force. It was so unsettling for me to know that we still rely on the power of death to protect peace.

I am in no way condemning the choices made by the US government to protect the Dalai Lama when he visits America. Nor am I suggesting how the Dalai Lama or Bishop Tutu should conduct their security. My critique was not for them; it was for me. It was for my own impulses to live a life of self-protection. I want to stop being guided by fear and believing the lie that force and violence hold the most promise to protect my well-being. Instead, I want to live in a world where the love and life of God are what make the world safe.

"Love is never the wrong way"[8] is one of the lines in a song we sing at my church. It is a great line, but it is a really hard thing to live.

We know God is love, so we ought to love. But it's hard to know what counts as love. Is it protection? judgment? confrontation?

It is rather surprising that with all the emphasis Jesus put on the importance of love that we don't have clear instructions for how to love. But maybe that's the point. To issue detailed instructions determining who, how, when, and where to love would take us back into the distinction-based, in-or-out If/Then trap.

The apostle John says it bluntly: "God is love, and those who remain in love remain in God and God remains in them."[9]

Maybe it really is this simple: God is love and we should be like God. We need to love others freely, without constraint or judgment. We need to love without deciding in advance that a person deserves our love. We are called to love in all ways and to love always.

Because love is never the wrong way.

Your Invitation to a Full Life

How to Stop Competing with God and Start Living in Integration with God

Go, your faith has healed you.

—Jesus

B y all accounts we live on a marvelous planet with utterly amazing diversity of life. It's even more incredible to think that our planet is just one small part of an ever-expanding universe that may be one of millions of universes.

From every angle, life is amazing.

From the most distant galaxies to the inside of an atom, from the unexplored ocean depths to the highest peaks, from the faces of newborn babies to the face of Leandra Becerra Lumbreras (who just turned 127), we see the amazing qualities of life everywhere.

Until recently I assumed that what made all this glory and wonder possible was that everything was just right and that balance was the key to life. I don't recall where I first heard that a perfectly balanced system was the key to life, but it sure is a prominent notion. It almost seems common sense that if things get out of balance—say, there is too much carbon in the air—the planet will heat up and life will suffer. Or not getting enough fiber in our diet can throw off our digestion. Get out of balance and bad things happen.

It's no mystery why it seems important that we seek balance. As this applies to our personal lives, we tend to work on maintaining order to keep the balance. We want to manage chaos. Don't rock the boat. Don't tip the apple cart. Don't make waves. Don't disrupt the status quo. Don't demand change.

Find balance and keep it.

It makes sense that if there is symmetry in all of creation, then we ought to have it in all the areas that humans can control. The problem is that it is not balance but *asymmetry* that makes life possible. I was surprised to hear Neil deGrasse Tyson, one of the world's most famous scientists, say, "It's shocking . . . that there is any matter in the universe at all . . . [that] any of this would exist: earth, the galaxy and the like."[1]

What's the Matter?

Why is it a wonder that there is anything at all? To answer that, we need to take a short dip into basic physics to understand how matter is made. If physics isn't your thing, don't worry; it will only take a minute.

Imagine for a moment that we could journey back to the start of all things, say 13.7 billion years ago, just after the initial spark of our universe. There would be no matter, just light. Light and energy would be swirling faster and getting hotter.

There would be a lot of action, but what would develop would be radiation, not the hard substance of matter. Here is the thing: the particles being generated by light have a charge to them—they are energy. (Remember, according to Einstein's formula $E=mc^2$, energy and matter are the same thing.)[2]

If you recall much from your seventh-grade science class or caught a few episodes of *Nova* on PBS, you might recognize the phrase "Every charge has an equal and opposite charge." In science parlance this is called the law of conservation of charge. It means that when you create something, you have to keep a balance of charge. If you start with zero electric charge, you need to end with zero electric charge. So at the start, when all these particles were being created by superhot light, they had to be balanced. In order to keep this balance, when all this energy was churning billions of years ago, it was generating particles with a charge and also anti-matter particles with the opposite charge. As science fiction–like as this sounds, half the universe is matter and the other half is antimatter.

This is where it gets really interesting. There is another law you might recall from physics class (or health class): opposites attract. Charged particles find their opposite, and when they do, they cancel each other out.

Maybe you can see the problem. If all stayed in balance, the particles of matter along with all the antimatter particles would eliminate each other. There would be no matter at all.

But things exist in the cosmos, so somehow there were more particles of matter than antimatter. While the whys and hows still puzzle physicists, they do know how much out of balance the universe is. In all that energy churning, for every billion particles of antimatter there were *a billion and one* particles of matter. A tiny difference for sure, just one to a billion, but every bit of matter, every tree, every bird, all of life came from this tiny imbalance of excess. The key to all life is asymmetry.

Asymmetry was not only present in particles billions of years ago; as it turns out, it is everywhere. It affects biology, chemistry, mathematics, linguistics, architecture, and even human structures. Everywhere we look, life is asymmetrical—just a bit out of balance.

The Positives of Being Out of Balance

I think it's great that the universe is out of balance. The thing about symmetry or balance is that it implies that all things are as they should be, that everything is settled. It suggests that if you want to change things, you are working against the proper order that keeps all things together. But if life is the product of imbalance and asymmetry, then we are not called to leave things as they are. Life does not comport to some kind of ideal stasis. In reality it's messy, it's changing, it's out of balance, and that is the basis for life.

I find this notion of asymmetry freeing. We can set aside the view that the world is fundamentally broken because it's imperfect. Rather we can see the world as being the ideal setting for life. We can long for things in this world to be right without feeling the burden to force the world to meet a perfect standard that will never be achieved.

This is what I hear Jesus calling for when he teaches his followers to pray to God, "Bring in your kingdom so that your will is done."[3] That prayer is at the heart of the human experience of life, the desire to strive for harmony with the life of God instead of exhausting ourselves trying to force conformity to achieve idealistic perfection. Living harmoniously with God does not mean that all will be perfectly balanced. Neither does it mean that we should accept the world as it is. We can live a proactive, co-creative life with God.

Wanting to See

The setting was dramatic and really uncomfortable. The beggar was breaking the rules with all his yelling. Beggars were a fixture in this city. They were allowed to sit along the streets, but they needed to follow certain rules. One was that they maintain an appropriate distance from passersby—no blocking the way or approaching people directly. They could attract attention by making quiet tapping noises with their small metal cups, but any direct appeal for donations was prohibited. Most beggars chose to keep a low profile not only as a way to follow the rules but because they found it was more effective. They would receive more money, food, or gifts by being humble and quiet. So they sat along high-traffic areas and hoped to be seen.

So on the day one beggar started yelling, he stirred up trouble. The situation turned confrontational. The more the man yelled, the more people around him told him to be quiet. This only led to his yelling even louder.

Compounding the confusion was that the man was blind. He was not entirely sure how many people were near him, how close they were to him, and if he was in danger. But he knew what he wanted—the attention of the man at the center of the crowd.

The gospel of Mark tells the story like this:

> Jesus and his followers came into Jericho. As Jesus was leaving Jericho, together with his disciples and a sizable crowd, a blind beggar named Bartimaeus, Timaeus' son, was sitting beside the road. When he heard that Jesus of Nazareth was there, he began to shout, "Jesus, Son of David, show me mercy!" Many scolded him, telling him to be quiet, but he shouted even louder, "Son of David, show me mercy!"[4]

The story doesn't indicate how Bartimaeus knew of Jesus or what he thought of him. Perhaps Bartimaeus tried to engage with all the traveling healers who came through town. Maybe his yelling "Son of David, show me mercy!" was a version of a "Will work for food" sign. He might have yelled it to all who would listen, just as a matter of course. Or maybe he had been waiting for months for the famed Son of Man to come to town.

There is a relational power dynamic in Bartimaeus's statement "Son of David, show me mercy!" It's as if he were saying "You have the power; I have the weakness." Perhaps this was a way of deferring to the status of the prophet. Bartimaeus could easily have been honoring recognized status and the social order and at the same time breaking the rules by yelling when he was supposed to be quiet. I like this guy. He knew that disruption is sometimes the only way to make change.

The crowd grew louder and told him to stop bothering Jesus. I can understand their response as well. They had a good thing going and didn't want a beggar—with his seemingly unchangeable need—to become a distraction. They had a lot of plans for Jesus, an agenda to keep. There was a balance in place, and the people wanted to keep it that way.

But Bartimaeus was like the particle that represents just one in one billion. His presence and out-of-bounds behavior knocked things out of balance, making it uncomfortable for the rules keepers. And as the crowd tried to keep things in order, trying to quiet the beggar, Jesus took the side of the disruptor.

Jesus stopped and said, "Call him forward."

They called the blind man, "Be encouraged! Get up! He's calling you."

Throwing his coat to the side, he jumped up and came to Jesus.

Jesus asked him, "What do you want me to do for you?"

The blind man said, "Teacher, I want to see."

Jesus said, "Go, your faith has healed you." At once he was able to see, and he began to follow Jesus on the way.[5]

I love that Jesus followed the lead of a blind beggar who was disrupting the crowd and violating the established rules. A beggar asked him to stop, and Jesus stopped. Jesus, the recognized son of King David, deferred to a rule breaker who occupied a low rung on the social ladder.

And then the story shows an even greater shift in the power dynamic when Jesus said, "What do you want me to do for you?"

The question tells us as much as the setting or the circumstances of the encounter. Jesus stopped: he honored a disruption by engaging the man in conversation. Then he asked the man to determine the agenda. The Gospels show this kind of thing all the time: those who are seen as outsiders are as central to the story as Jesus himself.

Bartimaeus said the one thing he wanted was to be able to see.

This might not at first blush seem all that shocking. I mean, what else would a blind guy want? But there is more, something honoring in this exchange. Jesus didn't set parameters for what the man legitimately needed. Instead, he asked what the man wanted. I don't think this a test question. Jesus wasn't setting the guy up for a Pass/Fail inquisition. Jesus wasn't acting like a kingdom of God border-patrol agent, making sure people answer the questions correctly before they are granted entrance.

Rather, Jesus's question cut to the heart of the call to live In God. Even though Bartimaeus was a blind beggar, one who had grown accustomed to being overlooked, he was first and foremost a human being. What he wanted mattered to Jesus. This is a story that reminds us that our desires, our passions, and our needs really do matter.

Jesus's question—"What do you want me to do for you?"—cut through the religious barriers of the day. The man's opening statement, "Son of David, show me mercy," was riddled with religious implication. Jesus was in the lineage of Israel's greatest king; Bartimaeus wasn't. Jesus had the power; Bartimaeus had the need. Jesus had the healing; Bartimaeus had the blind eyes.

So Jesus Flipped the accepted hierarchy. This is not a question of what the Son of the King wants. It's a matter of what you, a blind beggar, want.

The exchange between Jesus and Bartimaeus was a Flip on multiple counts. The beggar broke the rule that required him to remain off to the side, out of the way, and not interrupting those who passed by. Jesus stopped and honored the interruption. A prophet who claimed royal lineage deferred to the request of a beggar. None of this conforms to an If/Then transactional religious system.

The familiar If/Then arrangement has no room for such a disturbance of the accepted roles. A transactional system demands near-constant denial of who we are and what we want. That system tells us that we should be concerned with what God wants while setting aside our desires. It presumes that our desires are at odds with God's and does not leave room for the "what do you want?" story.

Following the Beggar's Way to Life

Jesus called Bartimaeus to a life of honesty. "What do you want me to do for you?" with no presuppositions. Bartimaeus was forthright about what he wanted. He desired to see.

His response was honest, passionate, and to some people's sensibility it might come across as less than humble. It was bold and direct, not self-effacing or self-denying. Bartimaeus would not have made a good ascetic.

Giving up your needs and wants often is portrayed as an act of devotion. The Christian tradition has an entire season of this, the forty days of Lent. It is a meaningful time for many people as they set aside what they enjoy. It is common to give up things for Lent, meat being a classic item to forgo. The choice to not eat meat, or at least to eschew meat on Fridays, is a long-held tradition dating to a time when meat was a highly valued food. To give it up helped a person to understand the sufferings of Jesus and the sufferings of others around the world. This tradition is still common among enough people that one of the first signs of spring is ninety-nine-cent fish sandwiches at fast-food restaurants. Other people give up chocolate, and others cut out smoking or carbs. Or they put the car keys away and hop on their bikes for the forty days leading up to Easter.

These can be beneficial practices that allow us to reset our patterns and to live with intentionality and conscious presence. That is a very good thing. But when these same practices are couched in a story of God that demands self-sacrifice based on the assumption that the pleasures in your life are necessarily the opposite of what God wants for you, then it is not a positive thing. The emphasis on giving up what you want is one of the beliefs that traps us in the sacrifice narrative. As in all things, we need to be reminded that God does not desire sacrifice but life.

I know people who are convinced that what God wants for you is everything you don't want for yourself. The corollary is that if God suspects you love something else more than you love God, that is the thing that will be taken from you. It will serve as a lesson in fidelity. Or they are convinced that their core desires present God with a problem. So God will want to strip each of us bare so we won't hold on to a desire or passion.

Other streams of belief ask followers to suffer to express their devotion. Some are so extreme they can seem bizarre, like the story of Sadhu Amar Bharati, an Indian holy man who, as a means of transcending his normal life, has kept his right hand raised above his head since 1973. The excruciating pain has now subsided due to atrophy and the loss of all use of his arm. This man serves as an inspiration for Shiva worshipers around India.

If we see our passions, our health, our desires as things God wants us to give up, we miss the call for the abundant life that Jesus invites humanity into.

How to Find a Better Way

There is a more subtle and far-reaching version of the self-sacrificing doctrine that I call spiritual deterministic complacency. It's not a phrase you will see on a bumper sticker, but it sure does stick in people's minds. It is the view that God's hand creates all situations. In light of God's active sovereignty over everyday events, we are called to accept the events. Slogans that support this view include "Everything in life happens for a reason" and "God will not give you more than you can handle."

Bartimaeus didn't buy into that line of thinking. He didn't say, "Well, I can't see, and that's a major drawback in everything I try to do. But, hey, 'I just want to let go and let God.'" On the contrary, he shouted, he ran, he caused a disturbance by believing that Jesus could do something about a problem that was keeping him from the life he wanted. And when Jesus asked him what he wanted him to do, Bartimaeus responded with the truth. There was no false humility.

Bartimaeus recognized that things were not as they were meant to be. He was meant to see, he wanted to see, and the right response to the question "What do you want me to do?" was "I want to see." Bartimaeus's desire was in fact a reflection of finding his life whole In God. There is no expectation that all people need to be the same or that all people who suffer from disabilities want them to go away.

As a person who lives with a generally well-functioning body, I tend to think that all people with disabilities would want to be healed. But that is not always the case. I was listening to an interview with Amy Purdy, who tells how losing her legs due to bacterial meningitis at age nineteen enabled her to achieve more than she ever dreamed. Eleven years after becoming a double amputee, she won a bronze medal at the 2014 Sochi Paralympic Games. Amy is a world-champion female adaptive snowboarder.

I was surprised to hear her say, "Eleven years ago, when I lost my legs, I had no idea what to expect. But if you ask me today if I would ever want to change my situation, I would have to say no. Because my legs haven't disabled me; if anything, they've enabled me. They've forced me to rely on my imagination and to believe in the possibilities."[6]

Amy founded an organization dedicated to introducing people with physical challenges to action sports. She has found life because of her circumstance, and she wouldn't trade that for anything. Bartimaeus wanted to be healed from his situation, but Amy found healing in hers.

How This Informs Our Living In God

I struggle knowing how to write this section because, on the one hand, I think the gospel calls us to be present in our own lives. We are to see our desires, passions, gifts, and lives as compatible with

God. I believe deeply that what the world needs are people fully alive, healed in all ways possible. The world needs us to live and love as ways to benefit and bless others. I believe that's what God desires. On the other hand, I don't want to suggest that God wants to fulfill all our narcissistic, me-first, me-only impulses.

There are times when we need to set aside our passions, desires, and wants in the interest of our own health and God's larger activity in the world. We need to align ourselves with God's hopes for all creation, sometimes at the expense of pursuing what is on our agenda at the moment. We are called to live harmoniously with God, ourselves, and one another, which often means pushing past a limited view of what we think we want. In truth, the bigger picture of what God is doing surpasses a temporary desire on our part.

And the key to this integration with God is being honest about what we want, desire, and long for. If we remain in denial of these things, there is little chance we will ever integrate our lives with God or the needs of others. Instead, we will live in self-imposed isolation from God.

We need to live in the tension of confidently asking for the things we need and desire while avoiding the trap of self-fulfilling narcissism. Too many people are so self-focused that they are convinced their every want is God's command. We need to find a way to not live in either extreme but in a new way.

Both starvation and obesity are a problem. We need to avoid death by starving our passions and also avoid the obesity of self-indulgence. People are dying of both obesity and starvation. In fact, there are more people suffering from obesity—1.5 billion—than undernourishment—925 million.[7] The solution for one is not the other. The solution is proper nutrition for all.

Similarly with desires and wants, it is the right thing to have wants and passions. The world suffers from people not living connected with their deep passions, passions that can lead us to create, invent, innovate, and invest in the well-being of others. But the world also suffers when we see *only* our own wants, pushing us to fulfill every fleeting personal desire.

This is again where getting the story right in our heads plays such an important role. It is easy for us to have a conflicted relationship with food, as just one example, to the point that what we eat or don't eat is done to fulfill other needs. It might be that eating a cookie is connected to a traumatic childhood experience of being caught in a lie or of being coerced into obedience because we wanted a reward. "Did you take a cookie from the cookie jar?" Or perhaps "Be good while we're in the grocery store, and you can have a cookie on the way home." So in adulthood, eating a cookie takes on a meaning far beyond eating a cookie.

Sometimes we develop comfort-food patterns. I have this experience with a McDonald's situated near some rental properties I own. For the last five years I have desperately wanted to get out of owning them. But with the current condition of the housing market, I am stuck being a reluctant landlord. I hardly ever want to eat at a McDonald's (other than every March when they bring out that Shamrock Shake), but when I have to take on my landlord responsibilities and I drive by those Golden Arches, I have a craving for fat and carbs. This happens at almost any time of the day. It's like some stress switch in my head flips and all I want is a salty, fatty, mostly beef patty.

Food triggers all kinds of emotions. Interpreting the feelings we have around food can get tricky; our perceived needs are different from our actual needs. The chemicals in food trigger certain synapses in our brains, and we try and make sense of it. It's easy to get a misleading message. Sometimes when we feel hungry, we are really dehydrated—it's not food we want but water. An intense chocolate craving can well be an indication that we are low on magnesium, B vitamins, or essential fatty acids. The deep desire for salt may be satisfied with a diet that is higher in electrolytes, but often we try to fill our yearning with something familiar, such as potato chips.

Before I started running and needed to pay attention to my body's nutritional needs, I had no idea that sometimes I needed minerals and not vitamins, or that the order in which I ingested food made a difference in how my body felt. I had so little idea of the chemical processing of food. I only knew to pay attention to the amount and some basic measurements of saturated fat. I basically had no idea what my body was truly craving. I only knew what I liked to put in it.

That is one of the beautiful aspects of the Bartimaeus story. It is a call to life, not to simple cravings or vapid wants. This is a beautiful story of a partnership between Jesus and Bartimaeus. Jesus pointed this out when he said, "Your faith has healed you."

Throughout this story we see no evidence that Jesus insisted on Bartimaeus first measuring up to a standard of perfection, morality, or devotion. Jesus didn't ask the beggar to deny his personal desires so he could be a worthy vessel. This was not a power struggle, a test of the beggar's submission to God's rule over the universe. Neither was it an If/Then proposition in which Bartimaeus would be required to give up something in order to receive the gift of restored eyesight.

The Bartimaeus story becomes the story of all of us. We are all reminded that what it means for us to be integrated with God is knowing what we want. Knowing the real desires, needs, passions of our lives and finding their integration with God.

We are called to know ourselves and to love ourselves. This requires trusting God and trusting ourselves. We are invited to see our life and faith not in competition with God but in harmony and integration, so that in faith we can live, move, and exist In God.

Who Is the Light of the World?

We Call Jesus the Light of the World, and He Says the Same About Us

> The light shines in the darkness, and the
> darkness doesn't extinguish the light.
> —the gospel of John

When our son was only a few months old, he needed more food than he was getting through nursing, so he was hungry most all the time. We were unaware of what was going on. His cries only seemed to be soothed by car rides, so I would drive him around at night, hoping he would stay asleep and I would stay awake. The pressure that comes from trying to help a baby fall asleep is intense. There is something about the incessant crying that made me feel like I was losing my mind. While driving around aimlessly in the middle of the night to help my son sleep, I felt like I was the one who needed to scream.

It sounds harsh, but in becoming a parent I had to come to grips with the sense of feeling trapped. This feeling doesn't go away quickly. As we raised our kids through childhood, life kept feeling small and predictable. I recall doing my best to be present while reading the same bedtime story for the seventeenth night in a row and not allowing my mind to wander into dark territory. I had to fight off the fear that this was all life was going to be, a repeating rhythm of *Goodnight Moon* and *Pat the Bunny* and *Oh, the Places You'll Go.*

Shelley, who was home most of the day with our two small children, experienced it even more deeply. A simple trip to the grocery store without a baby in tow felt like a "get out of jail free" card.

I was reminded of this feeling as I cared for my parents at the end of their lives. Sitting up through the night in their last days, helping them get comfortable, making sure they had water, and hoping they would fall asleep brought me right back to caring for our babies. At both ends of life, it seems, life is lived in the small, the simple, the ordinary. It's the small gestures that become the most important.

The in-between years can be filled with varying levels of what seems like a not-so-small life. On the grand scale of things, however, most of us live rather limited and simple lives. Even if we see ourselves as frequent travelers, we don't really go that many places on our planet, and the places we do visit tend to have been well traveled. No matter how much knowledge we acquire, we really know almost nothing compared to all that is knowable. There are seven billion people alive who have no idea we even exist.

Simply put, we are simple people.

And yet many of us also have a yearning for something more. We want to be part of something bigger than ourselves. We want our simple lives to have meaning beyond our first and last breaths. Religion and faith hold appeal for many of us because they give us a bigger story to belong to. That's why I think understanding that In God we live, move, and exist is such good news. It hints at what it means to be part of a grand whole, a never-ending story.

The Bigger Picture of Living In God

Even in the fog of the early days of parenting, I knew there was more going on than a massive shift in my priorities. Every parent knows the feeling of looking into the squinty eyes of a newborn or seeing a toddler explore the world or watching a teenager make difficult decisions about the future. The parent senses that this child is not just a freestanding individual, separate from the world. While she lives in a particular place in history, every child born carries the story and the biology of generations gone by. She will grow and learn and contribute to the ongoing story of her family and her community. She will add her perspective to the way that story is told. She will spread her DNA and life force through history. She is just getting her start now, but what shapes her and makes her was here ahead of her.

She is an essential part of it all.

I like the way my friend Michael Dowd talks about things. He has a way of opening ideas to their biggest frame so he can see the whole picture. He brings this way of seeing to history, science, and religion as well. Dowd calls himself a Big History evangelist. He wants people to see the grand narrative of life, science, religion, and all things. He has said, "Big History is a way to think about the history of the Universe and our place in it. Big History includes everything from the first few nanoseconds after the Big Bang to the birth and death of stars, the formation of our solar system and planet Earth, the emergence and evolution of life, and all of human history (including the evolutionary significance of religion and science) — right up to you now reading this."[1] I love thinking that the simple life we live is part of a grand story.

This is where I often find a rub with the way people discuss faith. So often, conversations of faith and Christianity feel like a small, specific story. Faith can feel limited, a lot like late nights with an infant where we are circling a room in the dark, trying to avoid running into the furniture, praying the baby will drift off to sleep. With the life of faith, one often feels that committing to one tradition requires closing our eyes to all the stories and ways of others.

That is another reason why the understanding of our life In God is so powerful. We find crucial connections where nothing is left out and no one is left behind. It is a faith that beckons us to the big, open story of God.

John's Testament to the Big Story

Poetry has a way of conveying big ideas with intensity and grace. The gospel of John opens with just such a poem. While the other Gospels include birth lineages of Jesus, John's poem is structured much like one of the Genesis creation narratives. The structure and vibe are big in scope, embracing the calling of all people, not just a select chosen people:

> In the beginning was the Word
>> and the Word was with God
>> and the Word was God.
> The Word was with God in the beginning.
> Everything came into being through the Word,
>> and without the Word
>> nothing came into being.
> What came into being
>> through the Word was life,
>> and the life was the light for all people.
> The light shines in the darkness,
>> and the darkness doesn't extinguish the light. . . .
>
> The true light that shines on all people
>> was coming into the world.
> The light was in the world,
>> and the world came into being through the light,
>>> but the world didn't recognize the light.

147

The light came to his own people,
>   and his own people didn't welcome him.
But those who did welcome him,
>   those who believed in his name,
>   he authorized to become God's children,
>>   born not from blood
>>   not from human desire or passion,
>>   but born from God.
The Word became flesh
>   and made his home among us.
We have seen his glory,
>   glory like that of a father's only son,
>>   full of grace and truth.[2]

Here, the life of God is framed not as a small, tangential story intended for a select few but the Big Story meant to include all. It's the story of all things having the same origin—the life that gave light to everyone.

The In-God reality in which we live, move, and exist is the biggest story possible. Over the last few years, when I have talked to people about this great interconnected story, I've heard a frequent concern. While people like the idea of setting aside the exercises of If/Then systems of faith, they worry that living In God calls for the loss of the personal nature of faith. As a friend put it, "'In God' sounds kind of Buddhist, like the individual doesn't matter. I have nothing against Buddhists, but the story of Jesus has always been meaningful for individual people, and that really matters to me. I want to have a personal relationship with God and not just be connected to others and to the universe."

I, too, worried that taking on the In-God understanding would cause me to lose all sense of personal identity. Or that God would lose meaning for me altogether, merging into a nebulous, faceless divine. I was not interested in embracing a soupy, vague, gray amalgam of humans, deity, and interconnected oneness with the universe.

The Big Story of living In God can easily be misheard as a transcendent reality that extinguishes the importance of each human life. If we are all In God, then what does it matter what I do? What contribution can I make that will stand out as having come from my individuality, my unique combination of talent and abilities and initiative? If everything gets lumped together In God, what's the point of taking risks and trying to make a difference in the world?

Surprisingly to me, just the opposite has happened. I have found that seeing each person as a full human being living In God has heightened the value of every person and his or her unique qualities and contributions to the whole. Rather than having to live with a complex system that has varying categories of "these people" and "those people" and "we people," each person is free to be a particular expression. Fortunately, we are always finding ways to make sense of the particular in the midst of the whole.

Understanding the particular in relation to the whole is a

dilemma of life itself. We have to consider it to make sense of our simple and short lives in light of human history. We cheer on each child born, even though there are four babies born every second on the planet. We honor every life as valuable and will go to incredible extremes to save a life even though more than 108 billion people have lived since the beginning of time.[3] We understand both the whole and the particular or, as the poem puts it, light and life.

Part of the Whole

I have found Jesus's statement "You are the light of the world"[4] to be one of the most inspiring, life-flipping things Jesus said. This deceptively simple statement has the disruptive ability to break the story of God wide open and allow it to make so much more sense.

Before we discuss Jesus's observation that we are the light of the world, let's talk about the nature of light. An understanding of light will help us also understand how something can be particular while also part of the whole.

The twentieth century was a bright time for light in the science world, and the advent of pop-science resources has helped novices like me understand a bit more about light. I will keep this simple because my comprehension of light only goes so far and because light can be a bit, shall we say, heavy. So first a couple of quick refreshers on the basics of light.

Light Fact 1: There Is No Difference Between Matter and Energy

As captured in the equation $E=mc^2$, energy is the same thing as matter and the other way around. In science parlance this is called wave-particle duality (wave and particle at the same time).

Albert Einstein captured this truth in 1905 in the $E=mc^2$ equation. While the equation is highly recognizable, it is a really hard concept to wrap our heads around. Before Einstein, entities such as mass and energy (and later time and space) were considered separate. But by bringing these seemingly unrelated elements together, Einstein gave us a whole new way to understand the world.

Energy and matter being the same thing is so counterintuitive to everyday experience that we still resist it. It seems obvious that the light shining on the table I am working at right now is different from the table itself. But while they are different, they also are the same. Crazy, isn't it?

Sometimes the most true things are really hard to comprehend. Like understanding how we are In God but also particular beings. What makes all this possible is that energy moves as particles and waves. Think about that: particles moving as waves. It really is quite amazing and resets so many of the distinctions we assume to be true about reality.

Light Fact 2: Things Are Made of Atoms

While there are many diverse variations of matter in the cosmos, at the atomic level, everything is remarkably similar. Everything that exists is made of only one hundred types of atoms. What makes a napkin different from the crumbs we wipe from our lips is only the particular combination of atoms.

Light Fact 3: All Atoms Are in Constant Motion

Atoms get even more interesting when we consider what they are up to. If you were small enough to get inside the paper this book is printed on, or if you could climb inside the glass and plastic of your e-reader, you would see that at the atomic level everything is in constant motion. Atoms are made up of the fundamental building blocks of electrons, protons, and neutrons. Protons and neutrons make up the nucleus of the atom, situated at a very small point at the atomic center. The electrons are outside the nucleus and move around it. Every atom is continuously moving and vibrating and rotating and flipping. At the core of life there is movement and change. It is only an issue of size that makes clusters of atoms seem stagnant and settled. In fact, the stability that we see in matter is the result of constant movement and change. The movement of electrons is predictable and consistent.

To put it simply, everything in the cosmos is moving. All the time. This wonderful wave and particle dance gives us new insight not only into how we live, move, and exist In God but also how our individual lives matter. We are In God, but we do not lose our individuality. We live as wave and particle. The two realities are not opposites in conflict with each other. Rather, they are crucial to each other.

A quick recap on light:

- Matter can be energy, and energy can be matter.
- Things are made of atoms.
- Atoms are in constant motion, and the motion is predictable.

That last bit about predictability is important for the making of light. The movement of electrons inside an atom follows a particular orderly pattern, and when an electron leaves its orbit and then returns, it creates a photon. When we see light, our eyes are absorbing the zillions of photon packets bouncing off items around us.

The key to creating light is to make change in the atom.

The key to light is change.

The way to get orderly electrons to change their predictable behavior is to add energy. Not only is movement important but so is interaction—energy engaging with other energy-produced light. The entire system can self-propagate: energy makes light, and light is energy.

If you are indoors, take a look around the room. If you're in a room with fluorescent lights, that light is made through adding energy in the form of electricity to the gas in the glass tube. Fluorescent bulbs contain mercury vapor, which is why you are not supposed to break them open. Electric current heats the gas and moves the electrons. Photons are generated, producing short-wave ultraviolet light that causes a phosphor coating on the inside of the bulb to glow. What you see as a glow is the result of energy and matter in movement.

You can add different gases with varying properties to produce a range of colors. This is what we see in neon signs. The different colors are the result of various chemicals with different electron patterns, and these patterns produce light in different places along the spectrum.

If you are in a room with incandescent light bulbs, the ones with coils visible inside, a similar process is happening. Energy is moving electrons, but not through an electric charge in a gas. Rather the energy is heat. An incandescent bulb uses a filament that glows and gives off light. These light bulbs operate on a principle similar to a fireplace poker getting red hot when it's left in a fire. As the metal gets hot, atoms in the iron are heated. This moves the electrons, which produces the lowest-energy light, so we see it in the red end of the spectrum. A similar effect is produced by the coiled wire in a light bulb. The coil is made of tungsten, which has a high melting point and can take a lot of heat. When it heats up, it glows with a high-energy, white-hot heat. And the bulb glows.

Light can be generated in many forms and for many purposes. One of the newest is light amplification by stimulated emission of radiation, better known by its acronym: laser. Laser rays are made by syncing or phasing the photons together through the use of mirrors and tubes. It produces a sharp band of light. This allows us to watch a DVD, cut holes to specification in various materials, and remove stubborn hair that grows in hard-to-reach places.

Light is wave and light is particle, and it manifests in different colors at different points along the spectrum. Light can be used for different purposes. You may already have made the connections between light and humanity and God. The more we know about light, the more space it makes in our thinking about God and humanity in participation.

This is why Jesus's use of light in talking about our place in the world is so interesting. Jesus was a big fan of using the understandings of his day to help people think about how to live with God: consider the mustard seed, the kingdom of God is like a woman who cleans her house to find a lost coin, you are like salt, and on and on.

If Jesus had spent his Saturday afternoons reading *Scientific American*, I bet he would have been even more excited about reminding people that they are the light of the world.

Finding Your Life In God

In the If/Then story of transactional religion, we are stuck with God being one essence and humanity being quite another. The two are said to be so different that something has to help them connect. This is not dissimilar to how people used to think about energy and matter, wave and particle. For a long time, common knowledge held that light and matter were different realities.

Light was understood to be only a wave and not a particle. Since waves are disturbances of a substance, scientists suggested there was a mysterious substance that allowed light waves to be transmitted. They called the supposed substance luminiferous ether. The false distinction of wave and particle necessitated the need for a transactional system.

The seeming pattern of distinction between energy and matter carried over into our thinking about God and humanity. So it went with body and spirit, life and death. But with a greater understanding of the nature of the world around us, we can begin to see how old constructs cease to be useful. Add to this the fact that no energy or matter is ever lost, only rearranged, and we have a great conversation partner to explore our beliefs about resurrection and everlasting life.

One with God

The twenty-first-century scientific understanding of light is one of the reasons Jesus's saying "You are the light of the world" is so provocative. His words remind us that we are a particle expression of God, visible in all kinds of colors and useful for all kinds of purposes. Our individual manifestations of that light are in the life of God, not distinct from it.

The first-century religious understanding of Jesus's reference to the light of the world is equally powerful and just as provocative.

When our twenty-first-century ears hear "I am the light of the world. Whoever follows me won't walk in darkness but will have the light of life,"[5] it sounds like a perfectly Jesus-y thing to say. But at the time Jesus said this, he was not universally considered to be an enlightened teacher or the Son of God. To many he was a renegade, antiauthoritarian preacher who was causing trouble among the masses and seeking to disempower abusive religious structures. While we might hear this phrase "I am the light of the world" as truth proclaimed by an unequaled spiritual teacher, the religious leaders of the day heard fighting words.

For a man to claim to be the light of the world was heresy of such a serious nature that it warranted capital punishment. The Bible records some of the outrage. A Pharisee objected, "Because you are testifying about yourself, your testimony isn't valid."[6]

The religious leaders were particularly bothered because Jesus wasn't coming up with his own, new metaphor; it was obvious that he was appropriating the familiar description of the first five books of the Bible, the Torah. In Hebrew, *ore* means "light," so Torah was seen as more than just books of the Bible. It was Torah that was known as the light that shows the way of life. Torah was the light of the world, not a run-of-the-mill country preacher like Jesus.

Jesus's making a claim like this about himself required a Flip of such magnitude that it's hard for us to appreciate it fully. Jesus was saying, in so many words, "What you saw only in Torah you now see in me." He might as well have said, "The ancient writings are not the limit to the way of life with God. The light of God that shows you the way of life is *me*."

The same imagery and challenge to familiar understandings is reflected in the opening poem from the gospel of John. Everything that was created received its life from him, and his life gave light to everyone. The light keeps shining in the dark, and darkness has never put it out.

This was so provocative that it caused a full revolt against Jesus. He said he was the light of the world, and he added that other metaphors reserved for the Hebrew Scriptures applied to himself as well. He said, "I am the bread of life," which caused some people to start grumbling because Jesus had said he was "the bread that came down from heaven."[7]

He kept at it, saying, "I am the gate"; "I am the good shepherd"; "I am the resurrection and the life"; "I am the way, the truth, and the life"; "I am the true vine"; "Before Abraham was, I Am."[8]

By making these claims, Jesus was not only making outrageous statements about himself, he was seeking to reorder where, when, and how God was accessed. He took images previously reserved only for Torah or the temple or for divine transactions and used them to characterize himself, who everyone could see was a man walking among them.

Jesus was suggesting that things that had been controlled by a system of If/Then religion were no longer limited to buildings and books and rituals but were manifest in him.

Flip.

And Also with You

Jesus stepped it up by proclaiming to people gathered in a field in Galilee that they were the light of the world too.[9] This blew the cap right off the If/Then system.

You are the light of the world. A city on top of a hill can't
be hidden. Neither do people light a lamp and put it under

a basket. Instead, they put it on top of a lampstand, and it shines on all who are in the house. In the same way, let your light shine before people, so they can see the good things you do and praise your Father who is in heaven.[10]

Let's pause for a moment to consider the revolutionary nature of what Jesus said.

You are the light of God! When people see your life they will connect it to God. This means humanity is connected to God. We have a role in revealing God to others. So shine, move, generate, create so people will understand the life of God.

We are light and we are called to shine. What a beautiful call. What a great way to see life.

We are called to let our light shine bright, to do what we were born to do. You are the only one who can live the life given to you. You have your own unique place on the spectrum, your own heat source, your own set of experiences, your own personality. If you don't shine your particular light, it won't be shown. But also know that it doesn't all depend on you. You are part of the Big Story. You and I each have our contribution to make, and we are not alone.

Among the great revelations of twentieth-century science is that every photon, energy emission, and elementary particle rings with its own wave signature. All of existence is energy, and it radiates, it emanates, it hums, it interacts. This is true of what comes into our eyes when we see a color. We are seeing a distinct frequency of visible light that appears to us as green or red or blue.

When we hear a sound, our eardrums are vibrated by subtle waves in air molecules around us.

The same is true with what emanates from us. The neurochemical processes of our consciousness, our thoughts, ring with their own distinct wave patterns. Brain imaging shows that our bodies and brains are in constant oscillation, synchronization, and emanation.

Recent studies of the interaction of neuron activity have made it possible to allow interaction between brain activity and computer electronics. Neural oscillations are being used as a control signal for brain-computer interfaces, allowing a direct communication pathway to be opened between the brain and an external device. While innovations such as placing electrodes directly on the surface of people's brains, allowing them to type simply by thinking about letters,[11] can seem scary and science fiction–like, it also is a fascinating way to understand what has been happening in the interaction of humans and all parts of creation since the dawn of time.

We also emanate waves from other parts of our bodies. Our hearts produce an electrical charge that can be measured with an EKG. Our bodies produce light that can't be seen with the unaided eye but can be seen with infrared cameras.

We're just beginning to understand the ways our individual bodies interact, emanate, oscillate, and communicate with all other living beings. These new understandings open fresh possibilities for considering what it means to let our light shine. We are all shining all the time. We are individuals yet part of the whole.

Reading Your Emanations

About fifteen years ago I had my aura read. I had no experience with such practices, but I did have a complete disregard for any "woo-woo" stuff.

I was at a neighborhood art fair, and I sat down at a table where a woman was offering free aura readings. I'm sure my skepticism was obvious, but she didn't allow that to become an issue. She said an aura is a luminous radiation field surrounding a person. She asked if I was interested in hearing what she saw surrounding me. I said, "Absolutely!" (I was starting a church in this neighborhood, so I decided to play along.)

She continued: "Your primary energy is coming from your heart and moving through your mouth. You are trying to tell of the life, light, and passions of your heart to others. The energy coming from your mouth is the kind that wants to attract and to heal." Then she looked at me and said, "If you are not yet organizing your life around calling people to join the passion of your heart, you should consider doing that. You have a unique spectrum coming from your heart and mouth."

I was dumbfounded. I had not even told her my name, let alone that I was to be a preacher at the new church around the corner. She knew nothing about my story but seemed to know me so well. In forty-five seconds I lost my skepticism. The certitude of dismissing something I didn't understand was gone. I was simply left with wonder.

I stayed near her table for the next half hour, trying to overhear what she was saying to others. She did not describe to others anything that came close to what she had said to me. Somehow, she saw something shining from me. I have wondered about this for the last decade and a half, and it comes to mind every time I hear Jesus saying "Let your light shine."

Living Life and Light

My friend Kevin lives with a terminal illness. While he is hopeful that his current treatment plan will be effective, his doctors tell him there is a great probability that he will not live more than a year. Kevin is making decisions every day about how he is spending the precious remaining days of his life.

At a dinner party at my house last week, Kevin told a few of us how he had just come back from Washington DC the day before. He had made a presentation on his work in the aerospace industry to staff and scientists at DARPA (an agency of the Department of Defense). We were amazed and intimidated by this, then surprised when he said, "But what was really exciting happened on Sunday, before I left for DC. We were at our cabin up north, and we discovered wild rice growing just around the bend from our dock."

His face lit up as he described his excitement during the process of researching how to harvest, cull, and prepare the rice. "While it was an honor to talk about those important ideas at DARPA, my soul felt so grounded and connected by harvesting that rice. That is what I really want to spend my time doing."

Ryan, who had just met Kevin, did not know he was ill. Ryan said to me later, "That Kevin is a really interesting guy. He just seemed so awake to life."

Ryan was shocked when I told him of Kevin's situation. But Ryan was right. Kevin did have a sense of being awake, enlivened, present to the moments of his life. Even with the prospect of death approaching much sooner than anyone wanted, Kevin was coming to life in new ways. We never need to be done growing the light and life in us.

Light, life, love. These make up the call of Jesus and the essence of Jesus.

Just as the opening poem from the gospel of John moves between light and life,

Everything came into being through the Word,
    and without the Word
    nothing came into being.

We are called to shine as we live, to let our light shine as part of the whole.

And the light gives life to everyone.

Free to Be

How to Find Complete Freedom In God

You will know the truth,
and the truth will set you free.

—Jesus

When I was growing up in the seventies, freedom was a big deal. It seemed to permeate my world, especially what I saw on television. I was raised in a family that loved TV. We watched sitcoms, cartoons, kids' shows, the news—it didn't matter what was showing. If any family member was awake, the television in our apartment was on.

Of the countless pixel-created memories of my childhood, four have remained vibrant. First, and the most powerful, is the "I'd like to teach the world to sing" Coke commercial.[1] The commercial provided me with my first television crush—the hippie girl whose face filled the screen as she sang. That commercial also made me a Coke guy. I remained loyal even through the cola wars of the 1980s.

The close-up camera shot was indicative of the era and created my second commercial memory: the public-service announcement that featured a crying Native American. The camera showed a man as he paddled along a beautiful river. But as the camera panned wider, it showed garbage floating in the water. The scene was punctuated by a narrator saying in a haunting voice, "Some people have a deep, abiding respect for the natural beauty that was once this country." The scene then changed to show the man standing on a city street with the voiceover "And some people don't." Garbage is then thrown from a passing car, landing at the man's feet. The screen fills with a tear running down the Native American's rugged, stoic face. The closing line was "People start pollution. People can stop it."[2] Even as a five-year-old, I wanted to be among the people who stopped it.

It wasn't only commercials that connected with me. The movie *Born Free* was about a lion cub being reintroduced to the wild. It included a song that became part of my childhood soundtrack: "Born free, as free as the wind blows. . . . Born free to follow your heart."[3]

The big daddy of TV influence had to be the ABC afterschool specials, including an adaptation of the record album *Free to Be You and Me,* featuring Marlo Thomas. These included poetry, sketches, and songs that stressed individuality, tolerance, and the importance of equality of genders in a way a kid like me could understand.

Add to the mix the miniseries *Roots,* news coverage of the free-love culture, the utopian music of youth culture, and the 1976 bicentennial celebration. My childhood media landscape was framed by messages of freedom.

It wasn't just a media campaign that made the desire for freedom important to me. As a fairly typical teenager, I had the constant nagging feeling of being trapped in my own body, which was constantly changing. The changes at times took a form I didn't like or understand. I felt trapped by my circumstances, where I lived, my friends, the rules at school, the acne on my chin, my inability to imagine a better life. I was trapped by my behavior and by things that happened to me that were out of my control. Like so many, I would sing along with songs on the radio at the top of my lungs, "We gotta get out while we're young . . . baby we were born to run"[4] or most any other song that captured this need for freedom.

Jesus the Freedom Rider

So at age seventeen, when I read Jesus saying "You are truly my disciples if you remain faithful to my teaching. Then you will know the truth, and the truth will set you free,"[5] I was all in. I wanted that freedom deeply. I would do whatever was needed to follow any teaching if freedom was the promised outcome. And this has not changed; I still will.

I have friends who have decided that living in the way of Jesus or holding any longer to any notion of God is not for them. I respect their decision, but for me there is a story of freedom In God that is increasingly compelling. It won't let me go, and I don't want to let it go. I'm not suggesting that only people who see the world the way I do are free, not at all. But I find the teachings of Jesus to be my best way to freedom.

I have found in three decades of pursuing this freedom that there are an endless number of ways to learn the teachings of Jesus. Humans have an incredible ability to learn, and most of that learning happens in the background of our brains. Learning the teachings of Jesus does not happen only, or even best, in formal environments. Remember, we live, move, and exist In God. So learning from Jesus can, and does, come from everywhere truth is found.

We all come into the world with great potential and built-in instincts and intuitions for learning the specifics we need for life. We learn language, ideas, morals, and ways of life from those around us. We grow and change. We deepen and expand.

Neurologists tell us that humans are learning in every situation, even right from the start as the brain develops in the womb. Researchers discovered that newborn babies cry with an accent that matches their mothers'. In a study reported in *Scientific American*, "a team of scientists recorded the cries of 60 newborns: 30 born into French-speaking families and 30 that heard German. And they found that French infants wail on a rising note while the Germans favor a falling melody."[6] We not only learn early, but our brain activity shows that we learn constantly.

Some of the most interesting discoveries in the field of learning center on mirror neurons. The words mean what you might think: neurons match, follow, or mirror each other even at the subconscious level. Mirror neurons make it possible for a person to have the same neurological and physical experience from watching something happen or from actually experiencing it. This could explain why a yawn is contagious. It also could be the key to how we learn a language by simply listening to it as a child. MRIs have shown that parts of the human brain act the same way when a person performs an action as when the person sees another individual performing that action. As far as the brain is concerned, we can actually experience something through another person. The triggering of these neurons also can happen through touch, sound, or thought.

Learning and knowing don't happen primarily by consciously taking in information and arranging it cognitively. We are much more sophisticated than that. We absorb, we mirror, we experience, we reflect. This adds great dynamism to what it means to learn from someone. All of this adds freshness to the notion that "you are truly my disciples if you remain faithful to my teaching. Then you will know the truth, and the truth will set you free."

There's an old parenting adage: more is caught than taught. This is not only true for children. All of us learn from the people around us, even when we're not conscious of it.

I was fortunate that the people who showed me the Christian faith emphasized freedom. We didn't talk much about neurological brain patterns, but they did use lots of Bible verses along the lines of "Christ has set us free for freedom"[7] and dozens of other passages about freedom. Freedom was a message that resounded in me as a teenager and does all the more today.

The Call for Freedom

A number of years into my personal freedom march I saw the larger context of how Jesus and the framers of the Bible used the idea of freedom and how crucial it is to living In God. The Jewish and Christian notions of freedom were woven into the narrative of the nation of Israel. We see this prominently in the Exodus of the Hebrews from Egypt. They were called to a living relationship In God, no longer burdened by the yoke of oppression and slavery. The way many Jews and most Christians in the first century talked about sin was the same way they talked about slavery. It was imperative that we be freed from it.

Sin was not understood as an offense against God but as any force that destroys and entraps humanity. So Jesus called humans to live the full life of God unencumbered by the cultural, social, personal prisons of slavery. People were implored to leave a life of sin because it caused human pain. Then and now, God wants people to live free from sin for the benefit of humanity. Living free from sin is not for God's benefit but ours.

This concept was not easily grasped by some of the religious leaders of Jesus's time. His statement "Then you will know the truth, and the truth will set you free" was derailed with a long argument over who was a child of Abraham and who was a child of God.

There seems to be an endless list of things that can trap and enslave us. There is a great piece in Alcoholics Anonymous's well-known Big Book known as the Serenity Prayer. This oft-quoted prayer asks God for serenity, courage, and wisdom.[8] Some things we can control and some we can't. That idea can be freeing, but much of the power of this prayer is in the line "and the wisdom to know the difference." There are many times we fool ourselves into thinking there is nothing we can do about situations in our lives. But that can leave us feeling powerless to invest ourselves in bringing about the change we want to see in the world. The wisdom to know the one from the other ought to lead us to see that much more is in the column of what we *can* change than in the column of what we *can't*.

There are times we realize there are no prisons or bars that hold us. It is only our own lives that trap us from freely following the life of God. The freedom we seek is found in opening our lives and letting go.

Perhaps you have heard of a phenomenon called the monkey trap. A fascinating BBC video shows how people who live in the Kalahari use an ingenious way to find water.[9] Finding water is, of course, key to survival, and this quest shapes nearly everything in the lives of the San people. It turns out that the animals that live in this part of the world are very, very good at finding water.

Baboons in particular have secret underground water holes they use to survive.

Because baboons are notoriously secretive and afraid of people, those hoping to follow them to their water source are out of luck. So San hunters get a baboon's attention by taking a large handful of melon seeds and waving them in the air so the baboon can smell them. Then the hunter digs a small hole in a hard mound of dirt and stuffs the seeds into the hole. The hole is just the right size for a baboon to get his opened hand and arm into the hole.

Then the hunter steps away to watch. The baboon is so tantalized by the smell of the melon seeds that he runs to the hole, squeezes his hand inside, and grabs a fist full of seeds. But with a clenched fist, the baboon can't pull his hand out. All the baboon needs to do is open his hand, let go of the seeds, and pull his hand free. But the baboon often waits too long. He is trapped by his own doing.

Fortunately for the baboon, the hunter has no ill intention. He simply wants to follow the baboon. The hunter puts a noose around the baboon's neck and ties him to a tree. He then feeds him large amounts of salt, which the baboon loves. The next morning, when the baboon is deeply in need of water, the hunter unties him.

Now the baboon is so motivated to get to his secret watering hole he's not concerned about his normal fear of the hunter. So the man follows the baboon to the secret water source that he could never have found on his own.

While in the desert these traps provide life for the hunter, it is easy to see the parallel to the times when we find ourselves holding on to things in our lives, be they beliefs, habits, anger, or pain, that trap us. It is much harder than it seems to let go of the proverbial melon seeds and free ourselves from the trap.

Freedom to Live in the Now

The point of freedom is so we can find life. One of the traps that catches many of us is the habit of living in the future. By living in the future, we are paralyzed by our current situation and find ourselves worrying about what might be. Freedom from this trap is found in living in the here and now. Jesus reminded his worried followers about this when he said, "Stop worrying about tomorrow, because tomorrow will worry about itself. Each day has enough trouble of its own."[10] While these simple words are rarely enough to stop a worrying mind, the power comes from the bigger idea that we are In God. Because of that, we don't have to feel trapped by the past or the future. The call is to not live in the future or the past but In God in the here and now.

As much as I want to follow the teachings of Jesus and find the freedom he promised, living in the now is really hard. Like a lot of people, I have a story in my head that says it is irresponsible to live in the now. We are told that mature adults plan for the future. This view is not completely flawed, but it carries some personal downsides. It puts me on the "living in the future" treadmill, constantly seeking what will be. Tomorrow never comes because there is always another tomorrow. I fight against constantly planning for and worrying about a range of possibilities. Like George Jetson, I find myself yelling, "Get me off this crazy thing!" I want to stop living in the future and start living in the now.

Being fully alive in the present requires me to turn off the parts of my mind that so quickly and naturally compare the now to the past or to the future. Running has provided me with a great way to build my capacity to exist in the present and live in the moment. When a person is running long distances, it is a really bad idea to start doing the math. Nothing good comes from thoughts such as *If I feel like this at mile eight, will I feel three times this tired at mile twenty-four?* The gift of running is the opportunity to drop the idea that you are running from anything or to anything and to be present in each moment with each step. You don't worry about what is next; you center on what is.

A couple days ago I was finishing a long run and was feeling really tired with about a half mile to go. This happens a lot, so I have developed a mental and verbal process to get me through to the end. I say out loud, "You are right here. You are not up ahead. You are not where you came from. You are here." I say this with each breath, making sure to breathe full breaths, which is tough to do toward the end of a run. To help calm my mind I pay attention to my feet hitting the ground on each step and thank my body for this moment right now.

Rather than allowing myself to compare the now with how it

should be, I try to live in the truth: I am here, I am tired. Right now. Without judgment.

For some people it is the cessation of activity that helps them live in the now.

A few years ago, I had the chance to meet the German theologian Jurgen Moltmann. He is a very smart man with great wisdom and thoughts on God, faith, and the role of Christianity in the world. I admire him greatly and would love to tap into whatever it is that inspires and fuels him. I was organizing a conference where he was the main speaker, and it was my job to get him to Chicago's O'Hare Airport for his return flight to Germany. I was really interested in what he did to keep his mind alive and his intellect so sharp. So I asked him how he was going to spend his nine hours on the plane home. Would he spend it reading books or listening to music? He replied in a rich accent, "No, I will sit and think about what I think about things."

I was in awe and inspired by how he could be as present as he was. Then I reminded myself that we are all different and we need different ways to be free.

A Quiet Mind

In 1995 I met Dieter Zander. When we first met, I was a fan. I had read a book he had written and admired the work he was doing in his church. I saw him as a pioneer, a role model, a risk taker. I drove from Minneapolis to Chicago to see him in action at his church. The ways he talked about faith, God, church, and people resonated with me. But also I was intimidated by him. He was leading a huge church community. He was talented, good looking. And he seemed to have ready answers for things that haunted me. I felt so fortunate to be able to develop a friendship with him.

Over the years we talked often about what we wanted to see happen in our churches and in our own faith. We worked together on national conferences and plotted ways to make change in the world. Dieter was a smart and ambitious guy. He was also a deep thinker with a deep soul. For a number of years that deep passion manifested in significant worry and struggle.

Then, on February 4, 2008, everything changed. Dieter suffered a severe stroke. Six days later, when he awoke from a coma, he couldn't speak. His right hand was too disabled to play piano or hold a pen. He says his brain felt foreign after his stroke. Losing the use of the left side of his brain meant he was going to be living an entirely different life.

I saw him a year or so after his stroke, and I was taken aback. I tried not to let it show, but I know it did. We walked along the streets of San Francisco where he had lived for eight years. I was not familiar with how to engage with a stroke victim who had lost the use of the language center of his brain. So I nervously talked too much. Dieter's whole life had changed. Years earlier my wife and I walked these same streets with Dieter and his wife, talking about our kids, marriages, and lives as Christian leaders. We had so much in common.

In those intervening years so much had changed. Dieter's sons were off to college, he and his wife had separated just before his stroke, and now Dieter was living alone. With half his brain not working.

With his limited language, he tried to convey what was happening inside by saying over and over in a stuttered, jolting way, "I good. Me and dog live together. I happy."

I believed him, but it was so hard for me to grasp how he could now be happy. Did he not miss the life he had enjoyed previously when his brain fully worked? I could not conceive of what my response would be to losing all that he had lost, but I was sure happiness was not the emotion I would be experiencing.

Then it struck me: perhaps that was the grace, that both sides of his brain were not doing their usual thing. The left side of his brain, which had been affected by the stroke, also was the side that processed judgment and worry and "how it ought to be" thoughts.

Dieter now was able to live in how life is, not how anyone thinks it ought to be. He had his dog. He had a simple job at Trader Joe's. He had his friends. He saw what was and not what was missing.

This past Sunday, Dieter shared his story and his wonderful photography at my church. In these intervening six years his brain has done an incredible thing. The right side has taken on some of the functions that used to be performed by the left side, including allowing him to convey his thoughts with speech.

He told how in his work at a Trader Joe's grocery store, he is responsible for the excess food, which he calls the spoils, and for cardboard boxes and general custodial work. He told about the wonderful people whom he loves and who love him. He reflected on how he used to lead thousands while speaking from a stage. He now says, "Years ago, I was a popular man. Now, my friends are small. Small is good."

And to hear him now say it, I can see the freedom he was looking for all those years ago. It was not a freedom to make something different on the outside only but freedom from inside. Dieter now says, "Before, God was my boss. God is my friend now. God says, 'Dieter, you are not going to work. Now, we play.'"

As he says this, the eyes of his listeners fill with tears. They also long to be content with God and to see life not as work but as play.

He went on to say that early that week, while cleaning a urinal, he heard God say, "Dieter, this urinal is holy." And Dieter said, "I laughed. Urinal is holy, that's funny. Then again I heard, 'Urinal is holy.'"

One of the effects of losing the spoken-language part of his brain is that other parts of his brain have become active. Dieter has become an incredible photographer.

With the help of a friend, Dieter put his story into words in a piece he calls "Kingdom of Cardboard and Spoils."

If I'm the king of all I survey, then I am the king of
cardboard and spoils.

My kingdom is a noisy, windowless room in the back
of a Trader Joe's grocery store. Here are the haphazard

stacks of empty cardboard boxes. Here is the giant box baler. Here are the shopping carts marked "Spoils," their wire frames brimming with still-good fruit, meat and flowers.

In Dallas Willard's book *The Divine Conspiracy,* he defines kingdom as "a realm that is uniquely our own, where our choice determines what happens."

My kingdom used to be a stage. A microphone. A piano, and an audience of thousands. My kingdom was a performance. A show. A sham.

Then came the stroke.

Now, five days a week, I arrive at Trader Joe's in the early dark, hours before the sun cracks the horizon.

I push my mop up and down aisles, sweep my broom into corners to collect the debris from the day before. The store is quiet, empty. There is one audience in this kingdom.

But that's ok, because I'm not performing. There is no Stage Dieter here. No superman seeking to wow the masses with feats of spiritual strength.

I'm just me. Just Dieter. The guy who mops the floor, who bales the empty cardboard boxes for recycling, who delivers the spoils to the Salvation Army.

There's something beautiful about this simple, menial work, though.

Take the food marked as "spoils," for example. It's all

still good. The fruit is good, the meat is good, the flowers are good. But they're not perfect. Anything that has an expiration date of today cannot be put out in the store for sale. And if a pear so much as rolls off the smooth green pyramid of fellow pears, it gets put in the spoils pile. It's not perfect anymore.

So the Trader Joe's employees fill shiny carts with all the perfectly edible imperfection and wheel the load back to my kingdom. My last task of the day is to load the van with spoils and deliver it to the local Salvation Army, where it will feed the hungry, who won't care at all that their apple is lopsided, that their hamburger is in the waning stage of freshness. They don't care how it looks. They just want to eat.

To me, this, here in the back room, this is what is real. Not the bright aisles of suburban shoppers making their menu selections from stacks of perfection.

I understand the spoils. I can relate. Because I, too, am spoils. Over, and over, and over again.

I used to be packaged as perfect. Back in the heyday of my church career, I was a shiny, unblemished apple. At least that's the image I polished up and displayed to the public.

But now, stripped of my talent, my stage and my six-figure salary, I relish the imperfection. I revel in the spoils.

As I break down these empty squares of cardboard, abandoned boxes that once held and protected food more valuable than themselves, I survey my kingdom and I am pleased.

I feed cardboard piles into the giant maw of the baler and chuckle to myself as I think, "I am recycled Dieter."

I am emptied and crumpled and stained and ready to be used again in a new way, in a new life.

Work was hard today. I am tired. The knuckles of my twisted right hand are scraped raw—the hand is numb now, so I don't feel it when I bash it against something harder than skin.

But you know what? It's ok. I come home after work and I think, "It's good today."

It's not a sermon. It's not a performance. It's not perfection.

But the cardboard is recycled. The spoils are feeding the hungry. And today I am thinking life is good. It's very good.[11]

Dieter is not the only one. There is a clue in his experience for the rest of us. A person does not need a stroke to experience a change in his or her brain. As we consider spiritual life, we know how crucial our bodies are. There are practices that can help us turn down the levels of influence coming from different parts of our brains. The way we live influences the development of our brains. It used to be conventional wisdom to believe that our brains are pretty well set by the time we reach adulthood. And the way we are wired is just the way is it is. But we now understand that with exercises and practices we can keep our brains active and even change our patterned neurological activity.

Jill Bolte Taylor tells of her experience in a TED talk and subsequent book called *My Stroke of Insight*. Part of the irony of her story is that Jill is a neuroanatomist who studies how the brain works. In 1996 a blood vessel in the left side of her brain exploded. Over the next four hours she phased in and out of the use of both sides of her brain. At times she was able to recognize what was going on.

In a TED talk, she held a real human brain in her hands and described the functions of the different sides of the brain. She said, "Our right human hemisphere is all about this present moment. It's all about right here, right now. . . . Our left hemisphere is all about the past, and it's all about the future." She says that our left hemisphere "thinks in language" and is the part of the brain that says I am differentiated from you.

Dr. Taylor goes on to say, "Who are we? We are the life force power of the universe with manual dexterity and two cognitive minds. And we have the power to choose moment by moment who and how we want to be in the world."[12]

In her book, she wrote, "Although many of us may think of ourselves *as thinking creatures that feel,* biologically we are *feeling creatures that think.*"[13]

We are people who live both in the interconnected life

of God and connected to all things while also living in the particular reality of the here and now.

Through practices of guided thinking, relaxation, breathing, and the like, we can see that people can change some brain activity patterns. It is possible to change our minds, to live in such a way that we learn new patterns. With our practices we can find ways to *live free*.

It all helps me to understand a bit more of what Jesus may have meant by "you will know the truth, and the truth will set you free."

Yes, the truth will set us free, free to fully be you and me.

11

You Can Run, But There's No Need to Hide

*Experience the Freedom of Living,
Moving, and Existing In God*

> I heard your sound in the garden; I was afraid
> because I was naked, and I hid myself.
>
> —Adam, a son of God

I have long wondered why, with all its downsides, does the If/
Then approach have such sticking power? It is not supported
by a clear reading of Scripture, it is not consistent with what Jesus
proclaimed, and it is an incredibly hard way to try to live your
faith.

I assume it must deliver an odd sort of reward. I think its
power has something to do with the transactional system letting

185

us off the hook and allowing us to hide. It goes something like this: If we can create a system that makes life In God more controlled, we feel we can keep God at a safe distance. By keeping the transactional system front and center, we take comfort in the assumption that God will do God's part and not show up uninvited.

In contrast, the idea that God is always present in every moment, without first being summoned by our prayers or our obedience or our sacrifices, can leave us feeling exposed. What if God comes around when I'm not prepared? To avoid such an unsettling possibility, we try to confine our relationship with God inside a predictable pattern. Doing so allows us to relax in the confidence that we've earned the right to keep God from interfering. We keep our part of the bargain, and the very least God can do is reciprocate.

It reminds me of a time when I was asked to help chaperone a dance at my daughter's junior high school. My daughter didn't want to go if I was going to be there. "Dad, I love you," she said, "but, c'mon, I don't want you in the gym while we are dancing and stuff. It is just so embarrassing." Keeping parents in their proper place is a primary goal of adolescents.

It is tempting for us to try to do this with God. I don't know anyone who wasn't a little thrown off when first told that God knows everything we have ever done and everything we have ever thought. I was a youth pastor long enough to know that teenage boys in particular find this a fairly uncomfortable realization.

When God knows everything we've ever thought or said or

done, then God is onto us. And if God is fully aware of the unending layers of our failure to hold up our end of the bargain, then God is probably not happy with us. At all. That's a major weakness of the If/Then religious system.

This is where so many people of faith get stuck, me included. In my earliest years as a Christian, I was pretty sure that every time something bad happened to me, it was because God wanted it to happen—to punish me, to teach me something, to force me into a more committed faith. This assumption was supported by just about every Christian and church and religious organization I knew of. It showed up in the language of "refining fires" and being "tested by God" and "God having a plan for me." Any pain or suffering or hardship in my life was handed to me by God to make me a better person. It was a view of God as the ultimate hard-nosed coach who would do anything to train us well.

In that system, we have two choices: work really hard to fit the system or work really hard to hide from God.

We Are Called to Grow, Not to Conform

I am convinced that the more we grow in faith, the more we will take seriously the Flips that come from Jesus's frequent refrain "But I say to you." The more we practice life In God, the more we will outgrow our perceived need for the transactional system. We will begin to see that the If/Then system limits our growth as people.

With the transactional system, it's common to equate growing in faith with a more consistent application of the rules. Growth is measured by greater devotion to the system. But if you think about it, you realize that conforming is not growing. Conforming is a preference for something tangible—a system that spells everything out. Living In God is the opposite of that.

The call of Christian faith is for us to become fully human, to be emotionally healthy, well-functioning people who can live well with ourselves, in generative grace with all others, and in harmony In God. Any system that purports to accelerate the process or to amplify God's voice stands between God and us and stunts our growth.

Growth and change are key to life. When we are born we are naked, living in total dependence on caregivers. As we enter the toddler years, we develop the capacity for language and recognizing connections between people and things. This is a stage where we begin to name things and proclaim what is yours and what is mine.

During adolescence, our bodies and minds go through an incredible degree of change. This is the stage when we become increasingly independent from our families, and this means finding new relational connections. Friends often replace our families as a prime means of having our emotional and relational needs met. This also is a time when many people begin to struggle with their feelings about their bodies. As the chemicals that spur puberty flow, they can leave a lasting mark on us. The feeling of not liking your body or feeling ashamed or embarrassed is nearly universal.

We are meant to grow through the angst and shame of adolescence, but it seems that the older we get, the harder it is to leave those stages behind.

Faith, Spirituality, and Maturity

Our faith and spirituality ought to help with this by encouraging and equipping us to grow and mature. The call to live, move, and exist In God is a call to that kind of maturity. It is the call to see that we are connected while remaining unique parts of the whole. We are vulnerable, yet we are safe. We are individual, yet In God.

But the If/Then systems of transactional religion keep us from transcending the stages. Much as we see a person's development from infancy to adulthood, we can see the call for all of humanity to grow and leave behind previous stages. I see the ancient story of Adam and Eve as a picture of humanity through the stages of growth.

The Adam and Eve story follows the classic creation narrative format with the man and woman representing all of humanity. At the start we see them created by God and living together in harmony, enjoying the food that grows freely. We could think of their life at first being similar to new infants, naked and dependent and cared for by God, the Parent.

Then they enter the toddler stage of Adam's naming the animals and the two of them being given dominion over creation. Anyone who has watched a toddler might notice the similarities to lining up all the stuffed animals with their special names.

Then comes the most famous part of the story, when adolescence blooms. Eve pushes back against the rules, listens to another voice, and breaks from the family. Together Adam and Eve eat from the tree of the knowledge of good and evil. This is when they become aware of their nakedness. They sew fig leaves together to cover themselves, to hide their most private parts. Like a teenager in the throes of rebellion, they convince themselves they can hide even from God.

The story then takes a turn showing how ridiculous the idea is that people can hide from God. The larger truth is found in the absurdity of God playing the role of a hapless character, wandering through the garden, looking for the people. As if God is saying, "I know I put them here somewhere."

The story goes on:

> During that day's cool evening breeze, they heard the
> sound of the LORD God walking in the garden; and the
> man and his wife hid themselves from the LORD God in
> the middle of the garden's trees. The LORD God called to
> the man and said to him, "Where are you?"
>
> The man replied, "I heard your sound in the garden;
> I was afraid because I was naked, and I hid myself."[1]

This is the story that shows the silliness of the prospect of hiding from God. Had Adam and Eve been left hiding in the trees, the bigger story of Genesis would have ended. But, instead, the two are called from their attempt at hiding and back into life.

Notice that it is not God who is hidden by the events in the garden. It is the man and woman who do their best to hide. God is the one who keeps looking. It is as if even from the start, even in these ancient Mesopotamian stories, God is not the one who is hard to reach. All this distance and hiding is in the minds of the people.

Getting Out from Behind the Trees

Even with all its mythos, this story conveys a powerful message: God does not want us to hide. Hiding stops the process of growth. When we hide, we end up staying right where we are. Hiding causes us to be stuck. This is why we must be done with the If/Then systems—they are just another garden of trees to hide behind.

Healthy spirituality is the end of hiding. Spirituality ought to help us become more open, more free, less fearful, less ashamed, less hidden, more known.

But being fully known by others or even by God can be terrifying. Many of us have worked a lifetime to become proficient at hiding certain parts of ourselves. Living secret lives from those closest to us is common. And when we get good at hiding, it becomes easier to hide truth even from ourselves. We can slip into convincing ourselves that staying hidden is the honorable thing to do.

Theologies have been developed to tell us we are not worthy to approach God. That God cannot look on us due to the fact that God is God and we are not. God is said to be too good, too pure, too holy for us, so when we keep our distance, it is a way to honor God.

This is a rationalization of the benefits of hiding. It works to help us feel good about hiding from God and from one another. I heard a man respond to his wife, who had pleaded with him to be more open, to share his life with her. He told her, "Share my pain? Now what good would that do anyone?"

The impulse to not burden others with our issues can seem like the considerate thing to do. But isolation only increases the pain.

Even the Righteous Want
to Hide Sometimes

The theme of wanting to hide and the fear of being known have long been part of the religious conversation. It was picked up by King David back in 1000 BCE when he wrote one of the most famous poems in the Jewish and Christian Scriptures: Psalm 139.

The phrases from this poem transcend religious usage. It frequently is used at funerals or in public gatherings when collective comfort is needed. David described the reality that there was nowhere he could go where God was not already there.

This poem gives many people comfort. But a year ago, my friend Elizabeth Flipped my thinking and opened new ways for me to see what was going on. She signed up to do something at Solomon's Porch that we call a soapbox sermon. These are ten-minute sermons on anything a person wants to talk about. These sermons are wonderful. Most weeks our community is surprised and moved by what we hear. Elizabeth's story had a major impact on us.

She is a therapist. She told us that much of her work is helping people open their lives not only to others but also to themselves. Many people live in such fear of being exposed that they keep a lid on their lives. She used Psalm 139 as an example of how pervasive this tendency is. Elizabeth suggested that for many people, perhaps including King David, this psalm is not as much a comfort piece as it is a dirge. She asked us to hear the psalm from the perspective of a person who wants to hide from God, who needs relief from God's ever-present eyes. Picture the words being written by someone who finds it frustrating that hiding is impossible. Even as much as we may want it at times, we are never outside the life of God.

She reminded us that while we can think of David as the great king of Israel, he was a guy with a complex background. He was a child prodigy who was chosen to be king as a twelve-year-old. He was a child warrior who defeated the most intimidating enemy of his nation, Goliath. He also was a lustful man who, to cover up his adulterous passion, had the husband of his lover killed. He was at once the "man following the Lord's own heart"[2] and the one disqualified from building the temple because he was "a military man and [had] shed blood."[3]

Hearing that even David had reasons to want to live in the shadow of his own privacy is powerful for those who feel they want refuge *from* God. But this psalm should also call us to refuse to give in to our fears by going into hiding. As we can see at the end of the psalm, David is full of anxiety. He doesn't trust his own heart. He still wants to kill the enemies of God rather than love them. Like David, when we stay hidden we stay stuck.

Elizabeth asked us to hear the psalm as someone who felt trapped by the ever-knowing presence of God. She invited us to hear King David saying, "There is nowhere I can go to be by myself, to be alone, to hide, and I want to; I almost feel like I *need* to." As she described this, my mind flashed with the image of a person in the beating sun of the desert with no place to find shade. Here are David's words:

> LORD, you have examined me.
> > You know me.
> You know when I sit down and when I stand up.
> > Even from far away, you comprehend my
> > > plans.
> You study my traveling and resting.
> > You are thoroughly familiar with all my ways.
> There isn't a word on my tongue, LORD,
> > that you don't already know completely.
> You surround me—front and back.
> > You put your hand on me.
> That kind of knowledge is too much for me;
> > it's so high above me that I can't fathom it.
>
> Where could I go to get away from your spirit?
> > Where could I go to escape your presence?

If I went up to heaven, you would be there.
    If I went down to the grave, you would be
        there too!
If I could fly on the wings of dawn,
    stopping to rest only on the far side of the
        ocean—
        even there your hand would guide me;
        even there your strong hand would hold
          me tight!
If I said, "The darkness will definitely hide me;
        the light will become night around me,"
    even then the darkness isn't too dark for you!
        Nighttime would shine bright as day,
        because darkness is the same as light to you!

You are the one who created my innermost parts;
    you knit me together while I was still in my
        mother's womb.
I give thanks to you that I was marvelously set
        apart.
    Your works are wonderful—I know that very
        well.
My bones weren't hidden from you
    when I was being put together in a secret
        place,
    when I was being woven together in the deep
        parts of the earth.

Your eyes saw my embryo,
>> and on your scroll every day was written that
>>>> was being formed for me,
>> before any one of them had yet happened.
God, your plans are incomprehensible to me!
>> Their total number is countless!
If I tried to count them—they outnumber grains
>>>> of sand!
>> If I came to the very end—I'd still be with you.

If only, God, you would kill the wicked!
>> If only murderers would get away from me—
>> the people who talk about you, but only for
>>>> wicked schemes;
>> the people who are your enemies,
>> who use your name as if it were of no
>> significance.
Don't I hate everyone who hates you?
>> Don't I despise those who attack you?
Yes, I hate them—through and through!
>> They've become my enemies too.

Examine me, God! Look at my heart!
>> Put me to the test! Know my anxious
>> thoughts!
Look to see if there is any idolatrous way in me,
>> then lead me on the eternal path![4]

This psalm captures the fear of intimacy with God and with others that so many of us struggle with. Our fear of intimacy is so great that we set our lives in safe places where we can manage what people know about us. Elizabeth said that for many of her clients, the intimacy of being fully known—including every fleeting thought—is just too intense. It is no secret that this is true of all of us.

This level of being known even by God is nearly impossible to live with. During Elizabeth's talk I kept thinking, *That's why we prefer the If/Then systems.* Transactional religion allows us to blunt the discomforting reality that we are fully known by God.

If You Can't See Me

As the sermon unfolded, I thought about the cat my family had when I was growing up. Phoebe would put her paws over her eyes when she was going to sleep on the back of the couch. My dad would joke, "I swear that cat thinks that if she can't see us then we can't see her." I imagined that in her little cat brain, Phoebe saw herself not just going to sleep but disappearing.

I envied that in her. Even as a kid I lived, as I suspect many of us do, bouncing between wanting to be known, seen, and loved and wanting to keep my life private, compartmentalized, and safe. There are times when we all would like to disappear.

It takes real emotional work to rearrange our thoughts to the point where we could gladly exclaim, "Examine me, God! Look at my heart! Put me to the test! Know my anxious thoughts!"

Elizabeth was onto a powerful truth regarding living In God. It requires faith and trust in ways that never would be considered in an If/Then system.

Most of us do not live with full confidence that if we were fully known—every thought, every past action, every impulse—that we would be accepted or loved. Most of us seek to protect ourselves from rejection and disappointment by living insulated lives. We might keep even trivial or slightly embarrassing things private.

As much as we might say that God is love and that God has only acceptance and goodness for us, most of us struggle to live as if that is true. A lack of trust in God's love can lead us to live bifurcated lives. One of the two is a spiritual life with God, in which we open ourselves to an extent as we ask God for help, direction, forgiveness, or healing. Asking for help involves admitting personal needs and failings. The other life is the way we relate to other people. That life, for most, remains closed. Rather than living in wholeness and being open both to God and to others, lives are fragmented and, for the most part, closed to anyone on the outside.

This morning I had breakfast with a guy who said his struggles are eating away at him. It doesn't help that he never feels safe sharing his life with anyone. He is a pastor who feels he needs to be "the one who demonstrates that the freedom of God is greater than my struggles." With tears welling in his eyes, he added, "No one can know that I am still struggling with these same issues all these years later."

The particulars of his struggles were not the issue. The crisis was the fact that his role as the representative of the power of God was keeping him trapped and hidden. Unfortunately, he was right about one thing. If he were to let his issues become public, he would almost certainly be fired. This type of fearful reality can keep any of us trapped inside hidden pain.

We need a new set of practices to match the new story that we are living In God. This truth changes not just our relationship with God but also our relationship with creation and with all other people. Living in a new way will require new ways to see and be seen.

Being Seen

Have you noticed how hard it is to make eye contact with people? You have likely noticed when someone *does* make eye contact with you. It stands out.

I asked people at a gathering to pair off with the person sitting next to them, even if that person was a stranger. Their task was to stand and face each other and simply look into each other's eyes. They were to maintain eye contact for one minute. More than half the people could not hold the other person's gaze for more than twenty seconds. Some could not bring themselves to do it at all. Those who lasted a full minute admitted that their eyes were darting about, trying to find relief. Some said they experienced such discomfort it physically hurt.

It struck me that many of these people could pray for a very long time with their eyes closed, but one minute of wide-eyed engagement with another person was much harder. In the reflection time afterward, almost all the people said looking at another person was not so difficult; it was the struggle of knowing they were being *looked at* so intensely. Try looking yourself in the eyes in a mirror. It is disquieting.

This might be why the human impulse when we feel shame or guilt is to drop our heads in order to avert our eyes. It's a way to feel like we're hiding. Some people avoid looking at pictures of themselves; others don't like to hear a recording of their voice. We all have our own ways to hide.

As those who live, move, and exist In God, we do have the capacity to take in the love and acceptance of God and to experience it with other people. But it often takes work to change patterns in our behavior. It requires growth, which can take a lifetime. We are not called only to see the life of God in the world, but we also are called to grow to the point that we can *be seen* by God and the rest of the world.

This often involves creating new patterns of intentionality and practicing them until they become natural. Recently I was talking with a fifteen-year-old girl who is a professional snowboarder and part of our church. She was looking forward to winter, when she would be working on a few tricks over and over so that "when the competition comes, I can do them without thinking about it." To live in a new way, we have to be willing to do something that feels so unnatural to us that it takes practice. By repeating a new way of living, eventually it will become natural to us. This is a testament to our ability to change and grow.

Learning to See One Another

Shelley and I have been married twenty-six years, and we dated for six years before getting married. We have known each other intimately for two-thirds of our lives. I have almost no memory of life without her in it. We live in the same house, sleep in the same bed, share the same sink. We are parenting partners and sexual partners. We have blended our incomes and life desires. As we continue to age, we might even start looking more alike. To paraphrase a line from the Genesis story, it is as if we two have become one.

Yet seeing her, paying attention to her, that's another thing altogether. A few years ago we suffered through a deeply emotional period and found ourselves drifting from each other. Shelley noticed my unintentional drifting, and it caused her to respond in ways that were scary to her and disruptive to our relationship.

We found ourselves in counseling and in conversations with others about how to change the incidental patterns that were causing us pain. We entered a period of intense personal examination and intentional time together. Shelley would ask me regularly during the time we were drifting, "Do you see me?" I would answer as truthfully as I knew how with a "yes," but the problem was I didn't know what she meant. I didn't even know that I didn't know. I was trapped in my limited understanding of what it meant to see Shelley. This became evident to both of us.

We decided to create intentional patterns. Often this is what it takes to form a new practice, even if it's somewhat forced and awkward at the start. Like new snowboarding tricks, the more we practice a new way of living, the more normal it becomes. That is when growth happens.

For us, that meant making intentional time for each other. For months, we would end the day by sitting together on the couch with a glass of wine to talk. I had heard from friends that drinking a glass of wine functioned like an hourglass. We would sit together for at least as long as it took to get through a glass of wine. If we rushed it, it would be a noticeable, conscious act of gulping. This practice of sitting and looking each other in the eyes and talking about what we had experienced during the day and what we were feeling was revolutionary. We have very busy lives and were doing all kinds of things together but side by side. What was lacking was face to face, eye to eye, soul to soul.

I created a little practice for us to do at the end of our couch sessions. It was totally awkward at first; it just wasn't the kind of thing I would do naturally. But as my friends in Alcoholics Anonymous say, sometimes you need to fake it until you make it.

Shelley and I would put our faces close together, and I would touch Shelley on each cheek with my hand and say "Hi, I see you" while looking in her eyes. Then I would kiss both her cheeks and her lips, pausing to breathe with her. We would hold our faces together until we synchronized our breathing. I knew I needed the physical practice of touching, moving, breathing, and talking to help me see.

We still do this practice each night, but without the wine. It has become our ritual of seeing: touch, touch, kiss, kiss, kiss, looking into each other's eyes, and saying "I see you."

May You Find or Make a Place of Being Seen

Creating a natural rhythm to life is what spirituality, church, and community are supposed to be about, and we need to develop patterns and practices to help us do that. This is a great part of the benefit of meeting together with others—to be shaped, to be coached, to be encouraged to grow, allowing us to experience the never-ending love of God and to experience that same love in one another. Some of us have those places and practices. Others are searching for them and perhaps need to create them in their families, their neighborhoods, their churches, their communities.

As we do this, we need to remain aware of systems, churches, and communities that breed none of the openness that is In God. Church should not be hazardous to your health. Spirituality should not take from you. Remember Jesus's words: "The Sabbath was created for humans; humans weren't created for the Sabbath."[5] This is true of all of our religious and spiritual structures as well. Relationships and communities are meant to be places where people build one another up in faith and love, places for us to be seen and to see others. Anything else, anything that causes you to hide, to run, or to close off your life should be set aside.

For some of us this will mean leaving the places or churches that cause us to hide. For others it may mean staying in those churches but changing the story in our heads and engaging in open, generative relationship—perhaps for the first time.

For some it might mean continuing deeper into the life-giving community you are part of and being willing to share even more of yourself with others. And for many it will mean searching for a community where you can be seen, where you won't need to hide, where you are invited to grow. This might be in typical religious settings, or it might be at a gym or a bar. You might find this in a therapy or support group.

However you structure your life, wherever you are, whatever you do, whoever you become, know that, even if you run, there is no need to hide.

For In God we live, move, and exist.

Notes

Chapter 1

1. Colossians 1:15–20.
2. Acts 17:28.

Chapter 2

1. Matthew 6:5.
2. Luke 6:29.
3. Luke 6:29.
4. Matthew 5:13–14, emphasis added.
5. Luke 18:22–23.
6. Kevin Murphy, "Missouri Powerball Winners Live Modestly, Give Back to Hometown," Reuters, February 23, 2013, www.reuters.com/article/2013/02/23/usa-lottery -missouri-idUSL1N0BN06S20130223.
7. "Boston, 1967: When Marathons Were Just for Men," BBC News Magazine, April 16, 2012, www.bbc.co.uk/news/ magazine-17632029.
8. "Human Mammal, Human Hunter—Attenborough— Life of Mammals—BBC," www.youtube.com/watch?v= 826HMLoiE_o.
9. Romans 8:38; Acts 17:28; Romans 12:2.

Chapter 3

1. Acts 17:22–25.

2. Acts 17:25.

3. Acts 17:27–28.

4. Acts 17:29–30.

5. "English Prepositions List," www.englishclub.com/grammar/prepositions-list.htm.

6. "Seeing in the Dark," Radiolab, October 22, 2012, www.radiolab.org/story/245482-seeing-dark.

7. Jay Michaelson, *Everything Is God: The Radical Path of Nondual Judaism* (Boston: Trumpeter, 2009), 17.

8. Acts 17:24.

9. Hosea 6:6.

10. Acts 17:24–25.

11. 1 Corinthians 6:12, 19.

12. Ephesians 3:14–21.

Chapter 4

1. I found this with a simple Google search, and it looked familiar. See http://support.apple.com/kb/TA31198.

2. John 14:20.

3. Romans 8:38–39.

Chapter 5

1. Acts 17:24–25, 28, emphasis added.

2. Hosea 6:6.

3. Micah 6:7–8.

4. Matthew 9:13.

5. Romans 12:1.

6. Genesis 11:31.

7. Joshua 24:2–3.

8. Genesis 12:1–2.

9. Genesis 17:3–8.

10. Exodus 3:14.

11. Genesis 22:1–2.

12. Genesis 22:2.

13. Genesis 22:9–10.

14. Genesis 22:11–12.

Chapter 6

1. Keith Green and Keith Gordon, "Asleep in the Light,"
   Universal Music Publishing Group and Warner/
   Chappell Music Inc., 1978, lyrics available at
   www.metrolyrics.com/asleep-in-the-light-lyrics
   -keith-green.html.

2. Acts 17:27.

3. Matthew 11:28–30.

4. Genesis 2:1–3.

5. Exodus 20:8–11.

6. Mark 2:27–28.

7. Mark 3:1–6.

8. John 11:47–48.

9. Hosea 14:2.

10. John 4:19–20.

11. John 4:21–24.

12. Mark 11:17.

13. Mark 12:41–44.

14. Mark 12:38–40.

15. Mark 13:1–2.

16. John 2:19–21.

17. 1 Corinthians 6:19.

18. Ganga White, "What If?" in *Yoga Beyond Belief: Insights to Awaken and Deepen Your Practice* (Berkeley, CA: North Atlantic Books, 2007), vii. Reprinted by permission of the publisher. See the White Lotus Foundation website: www.whitelotus.org/articles/poem.html.

19. Matthew 5:3–11, NIV.

Chapter 7

1. Matthew 5:48, NIV.

2. Paul: Philippians 1:6; Solomon: Proverbs 22:6; Paul: Philippians 3:12.

3. Matthew 15:11.

4. Matthew 5:43–48, NIV.

5. Matthew 5:45, NIV.

6. Romans 2:4.

7. Matthew 26:52.

8. "Love Is Never the Wrong Way" by Cory Carlson, 2012. Used by permission.

9. 1 John 4:16.

Chapter 8

1. "Nothing's the Antimatter," Radiolab, www.wnyc.org/radio/#/ondemand/122617.

2. This is basically what Einstein's equation $E=mc^2$ was all about. When light is heated, it creates particles of matter. In Einstein's equation, mass is represented by m and the speed of light by c (c refers to constant), squared (the superscript 2), and energy is the E. Because energy and mass are the same thing, this formula lets you know how much energy there is in a particle by multiplying its mass by the speed of light (186,000 miles per second) squared.

3. Matthew 6:10.

4. Mark 10:46–48.

5. Mark 10:49–52.

6. "Amy Purdy: Living Beyond Limits," TEDx Orange Coast, May 2011, www.ted.com/talks/amy_purdy_living_beyond_limits?language=en.

7. Tim Worstall, "There Are Now More Obese People than Hungry People," *Forbes,* September 22, 2011, www.forbes.com/sites/timworstall/2011/09/22/there-are-now-more-obese-people-than-hungry-people.

Chapter 9

1. Michael Dowd, "God in Big History," May 2014, www.thegreatstory.org/god-in-big-history.html.

2. John 1:1–5, 9–14.

3. Carl Haub, "How Many People Have Ever Lived on Earth?" Population Reference Bureau, October 2011, www.prb.org/Publications/Articles/2002/HowMany PeopleHaveEverLivedonEarth.aspx.

4. Matthew 5:14.

5. John 8:12.

6. John 8:13.

7. John 6:35, 41.

8. Gate: John 10:9; good shepherd: John 10:11; resurrection and life: John 11:25; way, truth, and life: John 14:6; true vine: John 15:1; "I Am": John 8:58.

9. See Matthew 5:14.

10. Matthew 5:14–16.

11. Charles Q. Choi, "Mind-Machine Breakthrough: People Type with Just Thoughts," Livescience, December 6, 2009, www.livescience.com/7997-mind-machine-breakthrough -people-type-thoughts.html.

Chapter 10

1. This 1971 commercial can be seen at www.youtube.com /watch?v=1VM2eLhvsSM. For fans of 1970s television commercials, here's a candlelight version featuring the same Coca-Cola jingle: www.youtube.com/watch?v =_zCsFvVg0UY.

2. See the Keep America Beautiful public-service announce- ment at www.youtube.com/watch?v=KF-U0dL-9K4.

3. For great photos of lions and the sound of Matt Munro singing lyrics to the title theme from the movie *Born Free*, see www.youtube.com/watch?v=Rb2Awn_dYTs. John Barry, "Born Free," Real Gone Music, 1966.

4. Bruce Springsteen, "Born to Run," Columbia Records, 1975.

5. John 8:31–32.

6. Karen Hopkin, "Babies Already Have an Accent," *Scientific American*, November 6, 2009, www.scientificamerican .com/podcast/episodebabies-already-have-an-accent-09-11-06.

7. Galatians 5:1.

8. The authorship of the Serenity Prayer was recently disputed; however, research has documented that Protestant theologian Reinhold Niebuhr (1892–1971) penned the prayer as early as 1937. For more on this, see Laurie Goodstein, "Serenity Prayer Skeptic Now Credits Niebuhr," *New York Times*, November 27, 2009, www.nytimescom/2009/11/28/us/28prayer.html?_r=0.

9. "How to Find Water in African Desert," www.youtube .com/watch?v=NxkvY2FZRQg.

10. Matthew 6:34.

11. Dieter Zander, "Kingdom of Cardboard and Spoils," Conversations, September 2012, http://conversationsjournal .com/2012/09/kingdom-of-cardboard-and-spoils. Used by permission.

12. You can watch Jill Bolte Taylor's TED Talk at https://www .youtube.com/watch?v=UyyjU8fzEYU.

13. Jill Bolte Taylor, *My Stroke of Insight: A Brain Scientist's Personal Journey* (New York: Viking, 2006), 19.

Chapter 11

1. Genesis 3:8–10.
2. 1 Samuel 13:14.
3. 1 Chronicles 28:3.
4. Psalm 139:1–24.
5. Mark 2:27.